A CANADA STRONG AND FREE

A Canada Strong and Free

Mike Harris & Preston Manning

THE FRASER INSTITUTE

Institut Économique de Montréal

2005

Series editor: Fred McMahon
Director of Publication Production: Kristin McCahon

Editing and design by Lindsey Thomas Martin
Cover design by Brian Creswick @ GoggleBox
Image for front cover: © Photodixk Red / Getty Images
Coordination of French publication: Patrick Leblanc

Date of issue: April 2005
Printed and bound in Canada

Library and Archives Canada Cataloguing in Publication Data

Harris, Mike, 1945-
A Canada strong and free / Mike Harris & Preston Manning

Co-published by Montreal Economic Institute.
Includes bibliographical references.
ISBN 0-88975-214-1

1. Canada--Politics and government--21st century. 2. Canada--Economic policy--21st century. 3. Canada--Social policy. 4. Democracy--Canada. I. Manning, Preston, 1942- II. Fraser Institute (Vancouver, BC.) III. Institut économique de Montréal IV. Title.

JL65.H37 2005 320.6′0971′09051 C2005-902097-0

CONTENTS

MIKE HARRIS

Mike Harris was born in Toronto in 1945, and raised in Callander, Ontario. Prior to his election to the Ontario Legislature in 1981, Mike Harris was a schoolteacher, a School Board Trustee and Chair, and an entrepreneur in the Nipissing area.

On June 8, 1995, Mike Harris became the twenty-second Premier of Ontario following a landslide election victory. Four years later, the voters of Ontario re-elected Mike Harris and his team, making him the first Ontario Premier in more than 30 years to form a second consecutive majority government.

After leaving office, Mr. Harris joined the law firm of Goodmans LLP as a Senior Business Advisor and acts as a consultant to various Canadian companies. Mr. Harris serves as a Director on several corporate Boards including Magna International, Canaccord Capital Inc., and ACE Security Laminates Corporation and is Board Chair of the Chartwell Seniors Housing REIT. He also serves on a number of corporate Advisory Boards for companies such as Aecon and Marsh Canada. Mr. Harris also serves as a Director on the Boards of the Tim Horton Children's Foundation, the St. John's Rehabilitation Hospital, and Vince Carter's Embassy of Hope Foundation For Children.

He is also a Senior Fellow of The Fraser Institute, a leading Canadian economic, social research, and education organization.

PRESTON MANNING

Preston Manning served as a Member of the Canadian Parliament from 1993 to 2001. He founded two new political parties—the Reform Party of Canada and the Canadian Reform Conservative Alliance—both of which became the official Opposition in the Canadian Parliament. Mr. Manning served as Leader of the Opposition from 1997 to 2000 and was also his party's critic for Science and Technology.

Since retirement from Parliament in 2002, Mr. Manning has become a Senior Fellow of two major Canadian research bodies (The Fraser Institute and the Canada West Foundation) and is developing a Canadian centre for building democracy. He is also a Distinguished Visitor and lecturer at the University of Toronto. In 2002, he released a book entitled *Think Big* (published by McClelland & Stewart) describing his use of the tools and institutions of democracy to change Canada's national agenda.

Mr. Manning continues to write, speak, and teach on such subjects as the revitalization of democracy in the Western world, relations between Canada and the United States, strengthening relations between the scientific and political communities, the development of North American transportation infrastructure, the revitalization of Canadian federalism, the regulation of the genetic revolution, and the management of the interface between faith and politics.

ACKNOWLEDGMENTS

We have a number of people to thank. The Fraser Institute's Executive Director Michael Walker was instrumental in initiating this project and a guiding light through the process. Fred McMahon of The Fraser Institute played a key role in coordinating the research effort that stands behind the policies presented here. Michel Kelly-Gagnon, president of the Montreal Economic Institute, generously lent us his considerable expertise, as did Peter Holle, president of the Frontier Centre for Public Policy. We owe a debt of gratitude to many Fraser Institute research analysts—in particular Jason Clemens, Niels Veldhuis, Nadeem Esmail, and Brett Skinner—for their hard work in providing the data we requested. André Turcotte's polling provided vital information that helped us focus our ideas.

We are grateful for Lindsey Thomas Martin's superb editing and design work, and Kristin McCahon's steering of this project through the production process. Patrick Leblanc of the Montreal Economic Institute did heroic work managing the translation on a tight deadline. Phil von Finckenstein and Leah Costello worked mightily in arranging for the unveiling of this policy document in Ottawa. Both Jean Marie Clemenger, Preston Manning's secretary and researcher, and Elaine Pritchard, Mike Harris's assistant, did exemplary work in keeping the project on track.

Of course, we take full responsibility for the ideas and interpretations presented here. While we have relied on the insights of many, we set the analysis and the policy choices this document reflects.

FOREWORD

We believe Canada has not yet reached its zenith – that the best is yet to come. And we believe that this will always be true. Canada is such a land of opportunity that the future can always be bigger, brighter, and better than the past, no matter how great our achievements have been.

However, we believe that Canada is being held back by an absence of national vision and ill-advised public policies.

To address Canada's need for a fresh vision and better public policies for the future, the Fraser Institute, in cooperation with the Montreal Economic Institute and the Frontier Centre for Public Policy, held roundtable discussions with interested persons in 2003, followed by a series of cross-Canada consultations in Halifax, Montreal, Toronto, Calgary, and Vancouver. The result was the collection of a number of insightful ideas on goals, principles, and policies conducive to shaping and implementing a fresh Canadian vision for the future.

We reviewed and expanded these insights, and developed from them the Vision Statement contained in this document. This Vision Statement was then provided to teams of Fraser Institute policy analysts with instructions to draft public policy proposals that, if implemented, would make this vision a reality.

This is the first of a series of publications that will describe the vision and policy ideas that grew from this activity.

Here, in this first publication, we present our Vision for a New Canada. We look at ways to unleash Canadians' drive and ingenuity by expanding freedom of choice, by challenging Canadians to take greater responsibility for the exercise of freedom, and by deepening Canada's practice of democracy. We will also present important poll results describing

Canadian attitudes toward freedom, responsibility, and policy options embodying these values.

In forthcoming publications, we will present policy proposals under four major headings:

- *Freedom, Responsibility, and Quality of Life* will present policies for improving health care, the environment, education, and other services important to the well being of Canadians.

- *Economic Freedom and Responsibility* will put forward policies to boost economic growth, generate new jobs, and provide the means for sustaining a high quality of life.

- *Democratic Freedom and Responsibility* will propose ways to deepen and broaden democracy in Canada, eliminating what many have called our "democratic deficit."

- *Advancing the Interests of Canadians Internationally* will propose policies for strengthening Canada's international trade position and our defence and peacekeeping capabilities, and for restoring Canada to a leadership position among democratic nations.

In the policy section of this introductory document, we will examine a key policy proposal from each of these areas, but with a special focus on health care, due to its immediate importance to Canadians.

We sincerely invite you to carefully examine our Vision for Canada, the principles on which it is based, and the policies proposed for making it a reality.

Mike Harris
Toronto, Ontario

Preston Manning
Calgary, Alberta

A FRESH VISION OF THE FUTURE

1 WHY CANADA NEEDS A FRESH VISION

When Canada was conceived as a nation, its founders had a vision of what our country could become and pursued public policies designed to make that vision a reality. The object was to create a strong, prosperous, and independent nation on the northern half of North America by creating an economic union and national market, adopting the constitution for a democratic federal state, protecting personal liberties and cultural diversity, building a transcontinental railway, opening up vast new territories, extending the rule of law, and developing independent trade and foreign policies to advance Canada's interests.

The work of the founders was carried on, and added to, by subsequent generations. In the twentieth century, Canadians participated in two World Wars in defence of freedom and democracy abroad. We welcomed immigrants from all corners of the globe to strengthen our economy while expanding our cultural diversity. We survived the Great Depression and laid the foundations of a comprehensive social safety net for our citizens. We helped create the United Nations and invent international peacekeeping. We entered into the largest bilateral trade agreement the world has ever seen with our closest neighbour, the United States. Canada was one of the most respected and influential voices in the world, with our words backed by real commitments of money, personnel, and national resolve.

Without a doubt, we have accomplished great things together *in the past.* But what now of the future? Where is that strong clear vision for the future that will unite and guide Canada for the twenty-first century? And what are the public policies that will make that future a reality?

Over the past two decades, our quality of life has declined relative to that enjoyed by the citizens of many western European states, for example in health care. In theory, we have universal access to quality health-care services but too many of our citizens now find themselves in long line-ups for services that are far from number one in the world (Esmail and Walker, 2004). Too many Canadians find themselves paying higher and higher taxes for fewer and fewer services and benefits.

Over the past two decades, our standard of living measured in economic terms has dropped relative to that of the citizens of the United States and developed Commonwealth nations except New Zealand. In fact, Canada has barely kept pace with major European nations, which have particularly suffered from poor economic performance in recent years. (See Figure 1 for a comparison of key nations.) The productivity of our economy, on which our jobs and international competitiveness depend, has not kept pace with that of our largest trading partner. Canada has had one of the developed world's worst productivity performances over the last 20 years, and barely outperforms Germany, which suffered a large productivity setback during re-unification. (See Figure 2 for a comparison of key nations.)

FIGURE 1: GDP PER CAPITA IN SELECTED COUNTRIES, CONSTANT LOCAL CURRENCY UNITS

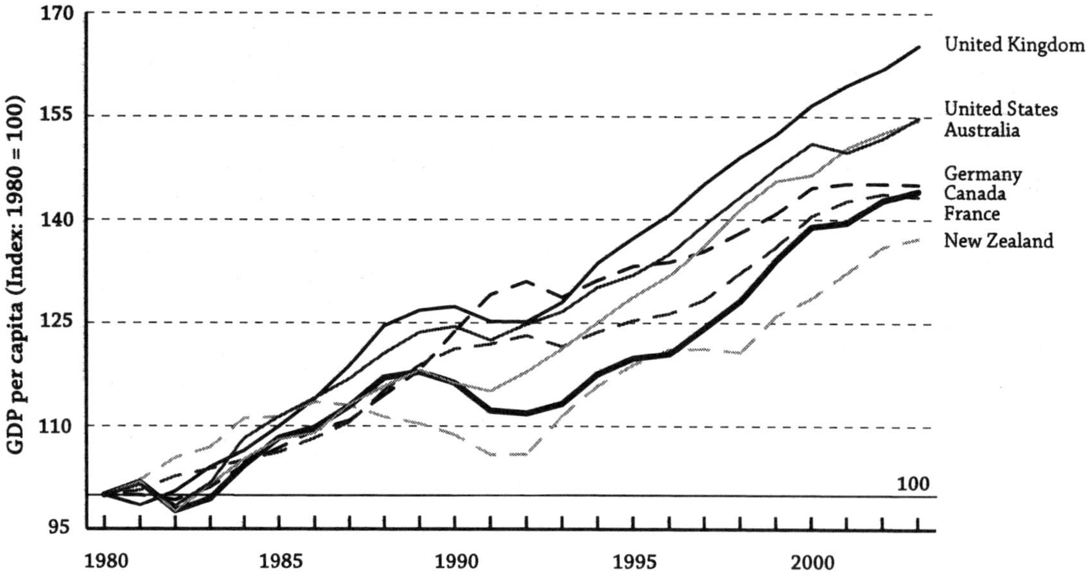

Source: World Bank, 2004.

FIGURE 2: MANUFACTURING OUTPUT PER HOUR

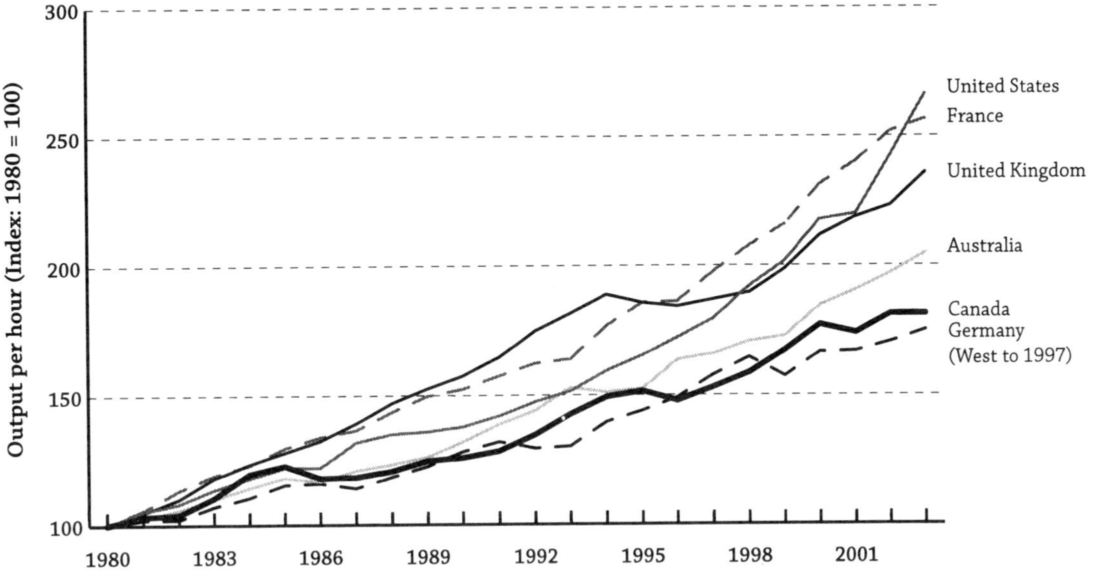

Source: US Bureau of Labor Statistics, 2005.

While we maintain the form and processes of democracy in Canada, the spirit and practice of democracy is on the wane in our country. Parliament, political leaders, and candidates for public office are held in contempt by increasing numbers of Canadians, particularly the young (see Figure 3a). Only 60.5% of eligible voters cast a ballot in the last federal election, the lowest electoral turnout in our history (see Figure 3b). The current federal government was elected with the support of little more than 22% of the electorate, and disillusionment with the effectiveness and fairness of federal institutions is again on the rise in Quebec and the West.

Our foreign policy increasingly fails to reflect the full range and depth of Canadian interests and values. Today, Canada is more known for its preachiness in world affairs and its diminishing willingness to back its positions with anything more than words and token support. Our influence in the political and economic capitals of the world—in particular, Washington, New York, London, Tokyo, and Beijing—is in decline rather

FIGURE 3A: PERCENT WHO VOTED IN THE 2000 FEDERAL ELECTION, BY AGE COHORT

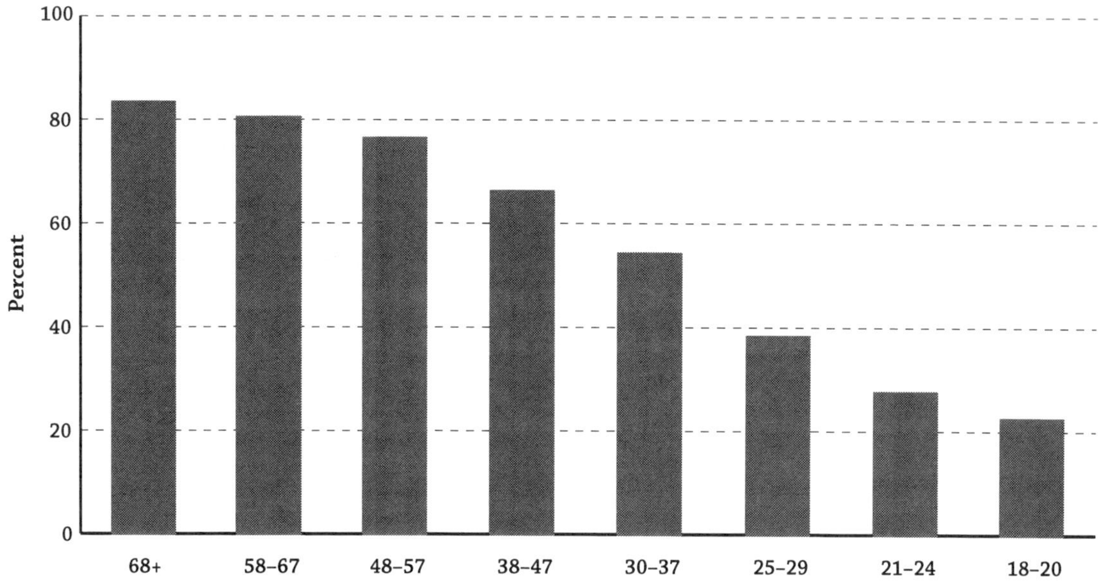

Source: Pammett and LeDuc, 2003.

FIGURE 3B: PERCENT OF ELIGIBLE FEDERAL VOTERS WHO VOTED, 1958–2004

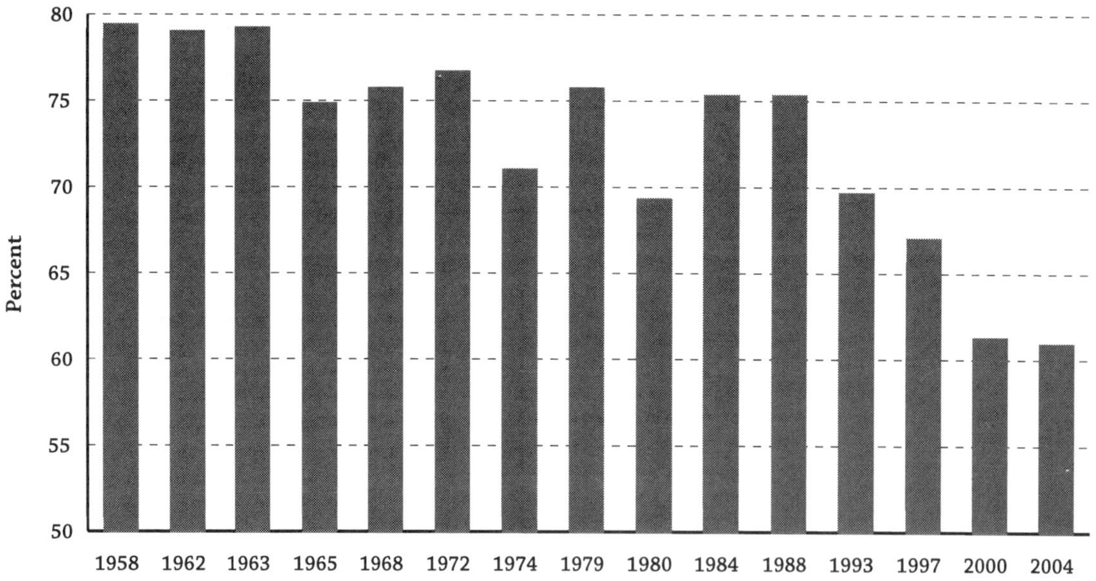

Source: Elections Canada, 2004.

than ascendancy, and the rights of our citizens abroad are increasingly treated with contempt by hostile states and rogue organizations.

The Canadian military, once a source of national pride, has for many years been starved of funding, equipment, and personnel. This is true whether the services are viewed in absolute size, size relative to the population, or military spending as a percentage of GDP.

- Canada's 52,500-person armed forces ranks 56th in the world, just behind Croatia and Sweden.

- Canada has 1.83 military personnel per 1,000 residents. By this measure, our armed forces are the smallest among the 26-member NATO alliance except for Luxembourg and Iceland; and 118th in the world, just ahead of Togo.

- Canada spends 1.1% of its GDP on the military—133rd in the world, tied with El Salvador, the Dominican Republic, Niger, and the Central African Republic. (International Institute for Strategic Studies, 2002).

A nation with the physical and human resources of Canada has by no means reached the limits of its development or influence. We are capable of achieving so much more as a nation—socially, economically, democratically, and internationally—than we have heretofore. The negative trends referred to above can and must be reversed, so that the Canada we leave to our children and our grandchildren will be significantly better and stronger than the one we inherited from our parents and grandparents.

In practical terms, it is possible for you and your children to enjoy a higher quality of health care, education, safety, and environmental protection than that currently available. It is possible for you to earn a higher income from a more secure job and for you to retain a higher percentage of what you earn than what the Canadian economy and tax system currently allow. It is possible to revitalize both democracy and federalism in Canada so that your voice and vote really count in public affairs and so that the vast majority of all our citizens in every region of the country feel truly accepted and at home in their own country. And it is possible to restore respect for Canada internationally, even to surpass the level of international respect that this country enjoyed following the Second World War, and to place the pride that all Canadians long to feel for our country on a more solid foundation.

AN INVITATION TO CLIMB

Just as Canada's first residents—the aboriginal peoples—would visit the high and sacred places of their territories to dream dreams and see visions of the future, you are invited to climb in your mind's eye to the high and inspirational places of our country and to look out on the horizon of what the future could hold for Canada and for all of us. You are also invited to examine the obstacles that presently prevent us from reaching that future and the policy paths that could take us around or over such obstacles. Your dreams, your decisions, your efforts are ultimately required to ensure that Canada embraces a fresh vision of the future and pursues it with vigour.

We sincerely hope that this document will prove to be a useful guide for that journey and invite you to share your vision, insights, concerns, and reactions to this document by visiting:

www.fraserinstitute.ca/strongandfree or www.fraserinstitute.ca.

2 OUR VISION FOR CANADA

THE GOALS

Our Vision for Canada embodies four high but attainable goals:

- achieving for Canadians the highest quality of life in the world;
- improving Canada's economic performance, so as to achieve and sustain the highest quality of life and living standards in the world;
- making Canada the best-governed democratic federation in the world;
- establishing Canada as a model of international leadership and citizenship.

ACHIEVING THE WORLD'S HIGHEST QUALITY OF LIFE

Quality of life means different things to different people. It may be defined and measured in terms of:

- services like health care, education, childcare, public safety, transportation, communications, and retirement security;
- physical environment—the quality of the air we breathe, the water we drink, the food we eat, and our relationships to the lands, forests, and animals with which we share this planet;

- relationships with others—spiritual, cultural, family, and community relationships, including our relationships with those less fortunate than ourselves;

- economic opportunities and rewards—more and better jobs and investment opportunities, higher incomes and more dollars in our pockets, better quality and choice of goods and services, and better value for our personal and collective (tax) expenditures;

- an effective voice in your government and influence over the policies that affect you, regardless of your province of residence.

It is precisely because quality of life means different things to different people that expanding freedom of choice, securing the means to exercise that freedom, and accepting the responsibilities that attend the exercise of freedom are all important prerequisites to achieving the highest quality of life in the world.

IMPROVING OUR ECONOMIC PERFORMANCE

Improving our economic performance is essential to providing Canadians and their families with the financial means—higher incomes from well-paid jobs and investments—to truly exercise their freedom of choice, make their own decisions about the future, reach their full potential, and accomplish what they want in life on their own terms.

Improving our economic performance is also the single most important thing we can do to provide Canadians with those goods and services essential to achieving the world's highest standard of living and quality of life. Without improved economic performance, Canada's present social safety net cannot even be sustained, let alone be expanded or made more secure.

Of course, "improving economic performance" must mean more than simply increasing Canada's per-capita production of goods and services. If environmental conservation is a fundamental dimension of quality of life—as we believe it is—then economic performance must be improved in environmentally compatible ways, not at the expense of the environment or future generations. (Environmental issues will be more fully discussed in future publications in this series.)

For the authors and contributors from The Fraser Institute, as for most Canadians, improving economic performance is a means to an end, not an end in itself. But it is a very important means, not one that can be taken for granted or subverted by poor policy choices.

STRENGTHENING CANADIAN DEMOCRACY AND FEDERALISM

Our Vision of Canada also means making Canada the best-governed country in the world – deepening our commitment to democracy and federalism and perfecting our practice of both.

Achieving this goal will mean finding new ways to ignite a "passion for democratic participation" among our citizens and to raise the level and quality of that participation. It will mean reforming democratic processes and institutions to improve their effectiveness and accountability as well as raising the ethical standards of political participants. It will also mean finding the right "balances" between the roles of the public and private sectors, between the responsibilities of the various levels of government, and between the conflicting demands of globalization and localization that will best enable us to achieve our full potential as individuals and as a country.

ESTABLISHING A MODEL OF INTERNATIONAL LEADERSHIP

Central to making Canada a model of international leadership is a refocusing of our foreign policy on advancing Canada's *interests,* including our national interest in exporting democratic and humanitarian values to other parts of the world and defending those values when they are threatened or abused. This also means reconstructing our unique relationship and influence with the United States, and rebuilding and modernizing our once proud military.

It means opening our borders for trade and removing barriers as quickly as possible. This will open further opportunities in the global marketplace and provide expanded opportunities for people from other nations to trade with Canada. This is immensely important in fighting poverty globally, far more effective in improving people's lives than foreign aid, which often only enables corrupt regimes to delay reform and reinforce their anti-democratic hold on power (see Gwartney et al., 2001; Devarajan, 2001; and Easterly, 2003).

THE CORE PRINCIPLES

We believe that the key to achieving all these goals is reinvigorating Canadians' sense of individual freedom and responsibility and achieving a better balance between the resources and responsibilities of the various sectors of society and levels of government. These principle-based initiatives will not only build prosperity at home and improve democratic governance, they will also make Canada a shining example for others and increase Canada's international influence.

More specifically, the three most important and principled prerequisites to the realization of our Vision for Canada are:

- a dramatic expansion of *freedom of choice* in every dimension of Canadian life—economic, scientific, social, cultural, religious, political—and in the world at large;
- a greater acceptance by Canadians, and better enforcement, of the *responsibilities and obligations* that attend any expansion or exercise of freedom;
- a strengthening of *democratic freedoms and responsibilities*, particularly through devolving power to the levels of government that are closest to the people, reducing the size and unmanageability of government, and

reforming the Parliament of Canada so it becomes an effective democratic forum for the people of Canada.

INTRINSIC VALUES ...

These principles are valuable in their own right. Individuals have the intrinsic right to determine their future course, make choices as they see fit for themselves, read and watch what they wish, associate (or not associate) with whom they please, bear the responsibility for these choices, and exercise effective democratic control over their own governments.

Freedom cannot exist without personal responsibility. As the state assumes more and more responsibility, our freedom and personal choices are eroded. When the state assumes responsibility for individual choices, it limits freedom. If individuals do not bear the consequences of bad choices, more people will make them and the rest of us will be forced to bear the burden. That, in turn, forces the state to adopt coercive measures to ensure that individuals make the choices the state considers appropriate, and liberty is even further eroded.

... LEADING TO SUPERIOR OUTCOMES

Freedom and responsibility are not just intrinsically valuable. In free societies, democratically governed and marked by personal responsibility, they have produced the dynamics that have brought the highest levels of prosperity, health, longevity, and education that this planet has ever known.

Individuals and families, given freedom and responsibility, simply look after themselves far better than government can. The drive and ingenuity of individuals in free markets consistently produce greater prosperity and lower levels of poverty than other alternatives. This is so clear from recent history, it is difficult to understand why the arguments continue that government needs to intervene ever more into our everyday lives and that government, and not the individuals who made them, must bear responsibility for bad choices.

EXPANDING FREEDOM OF CHOICE

When we possess freedom, we tend to take it for granted. It is when freedom is denied or restricted that we become more aware of its value and meaning to our lives.

In Canada, freedom is limited when monopolistic practices in either the public or the private sector limit our choice of goods and services. Barriers to the free movement and exchange of ideas, information, labour, capital, goods, and services limit freedom across provincial and national boundaries. Freedom is limited by poverty, discrimination, and segregation (as in the case of many of our aboriginal peoples), which deny people the opportunity or the means to exercise freedoms. Freedom is limited when the state commands too large a proportion of the nation's wealth and confiscates too large a proportion of the incomes of individuals and businesses. Freedom is limited when governments or private monopolies restrict scientific inquiry, lifestyle choices, freedom of expression, or the ability of people to act on their most deeply held beliefs. And political freedom is limited when one party, ideology, or viewpoint dominates the political landscape and voters are denied the opportunity to make choices among real public-policy options.

Expanding freedom involves reducing or removing these limitations and expanding the number, range, and quality of economic, social, cultural, and political choices available to citizens.

ACCEPTING RESPONSIBILITY

Freedom is one side of a two-sided coin. The other side of the coin is the acceptance of the responsibilities and obligations that attend the exercise of freedom. In Canada, while our Charter of Rights and Freedoms has emphasized and constitutionalized the freedom side of the coin, the responsibility side has been consistently and systematically neglected.

An expansion of freedom of enterprise, freedom of trade, and freedom of scientific inquiry needs to be accompanied by an expanded acceptance of responsibility for the social and environmental consequences of the exercise of those freedoms. An expansion of freedom of personal opportunities and lifestyle choices requires an expanded acceptance of responsibility for the personal and social consequences of those choices. Any expansion of religious freedoms needs to be accompanied by an expanded acceptance of the responsibility to respect the consciences and values of others. An expansion of political freedoms needs to be accompanied by an expanded acceptance of the responsibilities of citizenship and self-government.

Traditionally in Canada, fears about the real or potential abuse of freedoms by individuals or corporations have led to demands for heavy-handed interventions by governments and an expansion of the role of the state in society. But this invariably leads to a further curtailment of freedom rather than its expansion. To the extent that the practitioners of expanded freedoms will voluntarily accept a greater degree of responsibility for the consequences of their actions, this demand for state intervention can be lessened.

Our preferred approach to encouraging a greater acceptance of responsibility for expanded freedom of choice is to expand private property rights and the rule of law in such a way as to give a far greater number of individual citizens, organizations, and communities the tools to protect their own rights and freedoms when those are infringed upon by others, including the state. This approach is incorporated into the policy proposals of this document and expanded in future publications.

STRENGTHENING DEMOCRATIC FREEDOMS AND RESPONSIBILITIES

The exercise of freedom and the acceptance of responsibility are particularly important when it comes to the democratic governance of society. But citizens grow apathetic, indifferent, or even hostile to democratic processes (like elections) and democratic institutions (like Parliament, the legislatures, and municipal councils) when

- voters are not offered meaningful choices in elections or have little confidence in the fairness or effectiveness of the voting system;

- elected representatives are constrained by their parties or the executive arm of government from adequately representing and advancing their constituents' views;

- weak-kneed legislators deliberately surrender their responsibility for dealing with contentious issues to judges not directly accountable to the public, who actively seek to make laws as well as interpret them;

- regional and provincial interests are inadequately represented and balanced in a federal system;

- voters are unable to make direct input to government decisions affecting them or to discipline representatives who lose their confidence between elections;

- governments cannot be held accountable for their decisions and actions;

- voters have little confidence in the ethics of politicians or their willingness to tell the truth.

Strengthening democratic freedoms and responsibilities means reforming political processes and governing institutions so as to reduce and eliminate these deficiencies.

Citizens also accept less rather than more responsibility for democratic governance and the state of public affairs when

- governments are all too eager to do for people what they can and ought to do for themselves;

- the only exercise of self-government that the public participates in is an election every four or five years;

- public policies are developed and implemented by officials who are remote and distant from those affected by such policies;

- important public services are developed and managed by governmental bureaucracies remote and distant from the actual recipients of such services;

- responsibility for the provision of important services is so divided among different levels of government and among different departments of government that it impossible for the public to hold anyone in particular accountable for the quality and cost of services received.

Strengthening democratic freedoms and responsibilities therefore also means driving the making of public policy and the delivery of services, wherever and whenever possible, down to those levels of governmental organization closest to those affected by such policies and receiving such services.

OUR VISION IN SUMMARY

We therefore envision a Canada in which Canadians strive to achieve standards of living, economic performance, and democratic governance that are the highest in the world and enable Canada to be a model of international leadership and citizenship. We believe this future to be attainable through the expansion of freedom of choice, the acceptance of greater personal responsibility, a strengthening of democratic freedoms and responsibilities, and the implementation of public policies based on these principles.

3 REBALANCING CANADA

One of the positive distinguishing characteristics of Canadians is our commitment to "balance"—our desire to avoid extremes and find the right balance between alternative means and goals in various areas of personal and national endeavour. But, at present, Canadian public policy and its administration are characterized by several serious "imbalances"—imbalances that need to be corrected if our Vision of a better Canada is to be realized.

For example, in the provision of a social service essential to a high quality of life such as health care, all of the other industrialized countries with universal health-care coverage and health-care outcomes superior to those of Canada have "two-track systems," which strive to achieve an efficient and effective balance between the roles of public and private sectors in the financing and delivery of such services. In Canada, the monopolistic provisions of the Canada Health Act prevent this balance from being achieved or even pursued, restricting the Canadian health-care consumer's freedom of choice and resulting in health-care outcomes inferior to those of countries that pursue a more balanced approach.

A key objective in "rebalancing Canada" should therefore be to remove such obstacles and to implement policies that achieve a better balance between the roles of the public and private sectors in the financing and delivery of social services.

With respect to the structure and performance of the Canadian economy, Canadians need to re-examine the percentage of national income (Gross Domestic Product or GDP) that ends up in the hands of governments through public ownership and taxation—currently about 40%—versus the percentage that is left in the hands of individuals, families, business enterprises, and civil society to spend, save, or invest as they see fit—currently about 60%.

We believe that the key to higher productivity, better economic performance, and a higher quality of life is to increase the freedoms, responsibilities, and resources available to individuals, families, businesses, and non-governmental enterprises. A second objective in rebalancing Canada should therefore be to implement spending and tax reforms that increase the percentage of GDP held by individuals, families, and the non-governmental sector. A reasonable target would be to increase this percentage to 67% or two thirds of the GDP over the next six years.

With respect to the structure and performance of Canada as a federal state, another serious imbalance has been created through continued federal intrusion into areas such as health care that our constitution clearly assigns to the provinces. Expansion of the federal role in areas of provincial jurisdiction through the arbitrary exercise of the federal spending power violates the spirit of the constitution and creates needless strains in federal-provincial relations. It runs counter to the principle that essential social services are best delivered by the level of government closest to those receiving the services. And by increasingly dividing responsibility for the outcomes of social policy, it diminishes the ability of Canadians to hold any one level of government democratically accountable for social policy failures.

A fourth objective in rebalancing Canadian federalism should therefore be a devolution of power, responsibility, and revenue sources from the federal government to the provinces in these areas, as well as from the provinces to the municipalities where appropriate. This rebalancing need not "weaken the federal government" as some people fear, if it is accompanied (as we shall propose later) by a parallel strengthening of the federal role in its constitutionally assigned areas of responsibility such as defence, foreign affairs, and ensuring free inter-provincial trade.

With respect to the structure and performance of Canada as a democratic state, two further imbalances in our system of governance have resulted from:

- continued expansion of the powers of the executive arm of government (the Prime Minister and Cabinet) at the expense of the elected representatives of Canadians in Parliament;

- continued expansion of the role of the judiciary in the making of laws, again at the expense of the elected representatives of Canadians in Parliament and the legislatures.

A fifth objective in rebalancing Canada should therefore be to define more clearly and enforce more strictly the lines of authority between the executive, the judiciary, and the Parliament and legislatures, and to implement democratic reforms (as we shall propose later) for strengthening the role and effectiveness of Canada's democratically elected law-makers.

Finally, with respect to Canada's role in international affairs, a serious and embarrassing imbalance has developed between our national government's rhetoric and its actions on the international stage. As previously discussed, representatives of the Canadian government *talk* about our commitment to defending freedom and democracy from violent abuse abroad but our actual commitment to military spending (as a percentage of GDP), on which our peacekeeping capability depends, has declined to 133rd in the world. Canada, which by the end of World War II had the free world's third largest navy, today endangers its seamen and embarrasses itself by purchasing and operating second-hand submarines like the Chicoutimi. Our national government *talks* about its compassionate commitment to helping the world's poor but its actions do not begin to match the commitment of the Canadian people to that objective. The Canadian government's budget for foreign aid (as a percentage of GDP) is 0.26%, placing it thirteenth among the 22 rich OECD aid-giving nations, and its efforts to open free-trade doors for impoverished nations (the real answer to combating poverty internationally) are even weaker than its commitments to military and foreign-aid spending.

A sixth objective in rebalancing Canada must therefore be to develop the capability and commit the resources required to act effectively upon the verbal commitments we make internationally.

From time to time, even a good automobile needs to have its engine, suspension system, and tires "rebalanced." In Canada's case, the time is long overdue for striking a new and better balance between the roles and resources of the public and private sectors, between the various levels and arms of government, and between rhetoric and action on the international stage. We urge this rebalancing not for theoretical or ideological reasons but because we believe it will open the door to initiatives that will expand Canadians' freedom of choice and acceptance of responsibility, enrich our quality of life, boost prosperity, improve democratic governance and the practice of federalism, and increase Canada's capacity for international leadership.

ACHIEVING OUR VISION

4 THE POLICY ANALYSIS

What public policies, especially at the national level, are required to dramatically expand freedom of choice, the acceptance of attendant responsibilities, and the strengthening of democracy in this country? What public policies are required to allow that expansion of freedom and responsibility to dramatically improve our quality of life, economic performance, democratic governance, and leadership in the world? What public policies are required to correct the imbalances that cripple health-care delivery, that cause excessive taxation, that undermine effectiveness and accountability in government, that weaken Canada's international reputation—in short, what policies are required to rebalance Canada for the twenty-first century?

THE POLICIES THAT WILL DO THE JOB

The detailed results of our policy analysis will be discussed fully in forthcoming publications. But to demonstrate what type of public policy is required to maximize freedom and responsibility for Canadians, and how the adoption of such policies could dramatically improve quality of life, economic performance, democratic governance, and Canada's international leadership, we here present recommendations in four key policy areas that are essential to the achievement of our Vision.

We begin by discussing health care at some length because of its importance for Canadians. After diagnosing the current state of our health-care system, we will explore how federal intrusion into this key area of provincial responsibility has led to many of the problems in the health-care system and how respecting Canada's constitutional division of powers could restore accountability and responsiveness to the system. Health-care reform will also be further explored in future publications.

1 IMPROVING QUALITY OF LIFE—BETTER HEALTH CARE FOR CANADIANS

> *This equation of health care with the Canadian identity is unhistorical and untrue. We can't begin to have a serious, adult debate about the future of health care until we abandon the mantra that our national identity is somehow tied up in a state monopoly of health insurance ... The country was 117 years old in 1984 when the Canada Health Act created the current system by effectively outlawing private medical and hospital services.* (Michael Bliss)

There is a national consensus in Canada that health care is vitally important to quality of life and that no Canadian should be denied access to medically necessary services because of an inability to pay. Canadians may disagree about which policies are most likely to sustain and improve our health care but there is little disagreement over the objective itself.

We believe that the solution to providing better health care in Canada lies with the principles we discussed at the beginning of this paper. Canadians need more freedom of choice in health-care services. They should not be limited by a government monopoly over service provision. This holds even in areas where insured services are covered by government. Government and its agencies need not run hospitals any more than doctors need to be civil servants. Allowing Canadians to choose in this vital area will also allow them to assume more responsibility for health care by choosing the best providers for the services they want, not the ones government decides.

A key problem in health-care provision relates to our third principle, the importance of well-functioning democratic institutions. We believe the erosion of the ability of provinces to make policy in their own areas of constitutional authority has created many of the problems that characterize our health-care system. Thus, restoring provincial responsibility will lead to policies that enhance individual freedom and responsibility, and better health care.

The good news about Canadian health care is that Canadians are living longer and healthier lives than they were 30 years ago. The bad news is that while recent data shows Canada tied with Iceland as the number-one per-capita spender on health care among all the OECD countries with universal access health systems, we are not number one in any of the major categories used to measure the quality of health care provided (see Table 1).

According to a recent study, Canada ranks sixteenth in terms of doctors per capita (2.3 doctors for every 1000 Canadians), out of the 23 countries for which data is available. With respect to access to advanced medical technology, we ranked fifteenth of 24 in access to MRIs, seventeenth of 23 in access to CT scanners, and eighth of 22 in access to radiation scanners. Despite spending more on health care than any other industrialized country in the OECD (except Iceland), our citizens ranked fourteenth in the percentage of total life expectancy that will be lived disability free, sixteenth in infant mortality, eighth in mortality amenable to health care, ninth in potential years of life lost to disease, and sixth in the incidence of breast cancer mortality (Esmail and Walker, 2004).

Our diagnosis of the deficiencies of the Canadian health-care system focuses on its restriction of freedom of choice and misallocation of responsibilities. Our prescription for improving Canadian health care focuses on expanding health-care choices for Canadians and better allocating health care responsibilities.

The Canada Health Act (CHA) as interpreted by the current federal administration establishes a public-sector monopoly with respect to health-care insurance, requiring government financing and administration of all core health-care services and denying Canadians the opportunity to acquire such services from private providers. The CHA also forbids any user charges or extra billing for publicly insured services, thus preventing the use of pricing signals and market mechanisms in allocating scarce health-care resources efficiently. This government

TABLE 1: PERFORMANCE OF HEALTH SYSTEMS IN OECD COUNTRIES

	Mortality based on population statistics			Mortality closely related to the effectiveness of health care				
	Disability free life expectancy / life expectancy Rank 1999	Infant mortality Rank 2001	Perinatal mortality Rank 2001	Mortality amenable to health care Rank 1998	Potential years of life lost Rank 1999	Breast cancer mortality Rank 2000	Colorectal cancer combined mortality Rank 2000	Cumulative Rank
Sweden	9	4	7	2	1	1	4	1
Japan	5	2	1	3	3	4	3	2
Australia	2	16	9	7	7	3	2	3
France	1	10	17	1	11	5	5	4
Canada	**14**	**16**	**12**	**8**	**9**	**6**	**1**	**5**
Luxembourg	13	22	21	—	6	15	12	6
Finland	14	3	2	15	8	2	10	7
Italy	8	8	9	6	10	10	9	7
Norway	11	5	11	5	5	7	20	9
Netherlands	6	16	22	11	13	8	6	10
Switzerland	18	12	16	—	4	20	16	11
Belgium	7	14	19	—	18	12	12	12
Iceland	24	1	4	—	2	28	15	13
New Zealand	25	20	13	14	15	9	8	14
Germany	21	9	13	9	14	13	14	15
Korea	26	24	5	—	22	11	23	16
Greece	—	22	25	12	17	18	11	17
Portugal	11	14	6	17	24	14	7	18
Spain	3	6	7	4	16	24	18	18
Austria	10	11	13	13	12	17	21	20
Poland	14	26	23	—	25	22	22	21
Czech Republic	20	7	2	—	23	25	24	22
Denmark	21	12	—	10	19	16	27	22
Ireland	18	20	24	16	21	21	17	24
Hungary	23	27	26	—	27	23	26	25
United Kingdom	3	19	17	18	20	19	19	25
Slovak Republic	14	24	20	—	26	26	25	27
Turkey	—	28	—	—	—	27	28	—

Sources: WHO, 2000; OECD, 2003; Ferlay et al., 2001; Nolte and McKee, 2003. Previously published as Exsum Table 1 (page 8) in Esmail and Walker, 2004.

monopoly and associated restrictions lead to a very inefficient and wasteful system that denies timely health care to all but those with connections or personal wealth.

No other country in the developed world—even those with highly socialistic governments—goes to such lengths to limit freedom in its health-care system, restrict personal choice and responsibility, and insist on a government-planned monopoly regardless of cost.

Do the monopolistic and anti-market provisions of the Canada Health Act result in better health care? Based on international comparisons, the answer is emphatically "*No!*" Among the OECD countries with universal access systems, all of the countries that have fewer years of life lost to disease and that have lower mortality amenable to health care than Canada also have private alternatives to the public health-care system. And only one country in the latter comparison does not have some form of user fees at the point of access. Furthermore, not one of these countries spends more on health care than Canada after adjusting for a nation's age profile, a necessary step since the cost of health care varies considerably with a person's age. All of the countries that produce a greater proportion of disability-free life expectancy for their populations have a private care sector competing to meet patient needs, and over three quarters of them also have some form of cost sharing for access to the system. Looking at a specific, treatable, catastrophic disease such as breast cancer, Canada ranks sixth in mortality from breast cancer. All of the comprehensive, universal-access countries that do better than Canada in preventing mortality from breast cancer have private health-care alternatives and some form of user fees at the point of access, and spend less of their GDP on health care.

When we investigate the manner in which Canada allocates responsibility for health and health care, we again find major deficiencies but also great opportunities for improvement. Health-care needs and preferences are specific to individuals, families, and communities, making it extremely difficult, if not impossible, for governments to aggregate and optimally manage the different needs and preferences of millions of health-care consumers. It is informed individuals, families, and local communities themselves that are best able to determine their own health-care needs and manage their health-care choices. Likewise, it is the health-care providers and administrators who are closest to those informed individuals, families, and communities who are best able to respond effectively to their needs and preferences.

In Canada, however, our health-care system provides no incentives or rewards to individuals and families who practise illness prevention or healthy lifestyles, and little in the way of pricing signals to guide individuals, families, or communities in their health-care demands and choices. Health-care providers get most of their revenues from governments rather than the health-care consumers they ostensibly serve, rendering them more responsive to bureaucratic direction from above than consumer demand from below. Governmental bureaucracies are exercising more control over health care while individuals, families, and communities are exercising less. The result? Inferior, more expensive services and unacceptable waiting times for medically necessary services.

When individuals and families have choices in health care—as they do in virtually every developed nation on the planet except Canada—they can hold health providers directly accountable. That's not possible under Canada's government monopoly. Nothing better illustrates the perversity of our health-care system than the fact that in Canada "accountability" in health care does not mean accountability of the providers to the patients but rather accountability to two levels of government.

Envisioning for Canadians the highest quality of life in the world, recognizing that better health care is a priority aspect of improved quality of life, and believing that Canadian health care can best be improved by increasing freedom of choice and re-allocating health-care responsibilities, we therefore offer the following policy recommendations:

- Remove jurisdictional roadblocks to better health care for patients by substantially amending or replacing the Canada Health Act and transferring responsibility for health-care delivery and financing, including federal tax points, entirely to the provinces. Make Freedom of Choice a fundamental principle of any future health-care legislation.

- Expand health-care facilities and cut waiting times by removing all federal restrictions that prevent provincial governments from using private capital, non-governmental providers, and market-based pricing mechanisms in the development of health-care facilities and the delivery of health-care services to Canadians.

- Focus federal support for health care in the areas where it can do the most good: health-care science and research, no-strings-attached equalization payments to have-not provinces to enable them to meet national standards, and the collection and dissemination to health-care users of information on the performance of the Canadian health-care system including the portability of benefits between provinces.

- Reduce the federal personal income-tax rate from 16% to 15% for the lowest bracket, eliminate the next two brackets, and reduce the top rate from 29% to 25%. The reduction and elimination of these brackets would equal the current federal spending on health care and allow the provinces expanded tax room to finance health care. Note that the equalization formula will provide additional revenues to those lower income provinces for which a "tax point" is worth less than for higher income provinces.

In other words, we advocate freeing up the provinces and the private sector to innovate in order to resolve the current health-care crisis and meet future health-care needs. Health-care systems around the world—for example, the health-care systems of Sweden, Japan, Australia, and France—allow more individual freedom and responsibility while at the same time guaranteeing everyone, regardless of income, access to high levels of care. National health-care standards will be set by inter-provincial agreement through the new Council of the Federation, with federal equalization payments assisting have-not provinces to meet those standards.

What will the adoption of these measures mean to you and your family in practical terms? Most importantly, you and your family will be fully insured against catastrophic illness, just as you are now, and will have continued access to all medically necessary services regardless of ability to pay. These features of our current system will not only be retained. They will be made far more sustainable.

But in addition, you will have more choice in health-care services resulting in shorter waiting times, access to the latest medical technology, and better care. In most provinces, when you are sick you will still most likely enter the health-care system through the door to a doctor's office, clinic, or a hospital that is part of the public health-care system. But if your needs cannot be attended to promptly or satisfactorily, you will have the option of being referred to another facility offering equivalent or more specialized care where you can be treated sooner, and that facility, while licensed by the government, may well be financed and operated by a qualified private operator. If the services provided by the private facility are core services covered by your provincial health-care insurance plan, upon presentation of your Health Care Card the cost of your treatment will be covered by the province in accordance with the same fee schedule used at publicly run facilities. If the services you require or desire are not covered by your provincial health-care insurance plan, they may be paid for directly or through any private supplementary health-care insurance plan (which is the case now).

In addition to more choice in health-care services you may also be presented with obligations and incentives to assume more personal responsibility for your own health and well being. This will likely take the form of more "cost sharing" between yourself and the province for some of your health care through a combination of user fees, insurance premiums, deductibles, and co-payments. Cost sharing will make health-care users more aware of the costs associated with alternative services and more discriminating in their health-care demands and choices. Greater use of health-care insurance premiums will allow insurers to offer incentives (lower premiums) to those who look after their own health better than others, and allow governments to subsidize more selectively the health-care costs of certain classes of consumers (such as lower-income families and seniors).

As the freedom and accountability of provinces and health-care providers to reform health care is increased, we believe that Canadians in every province will benefit from the gradual adoption of those reforms that prove most effective in improving timely access to high quality care. As your freedom of choice and acceptance of responsibility with respect to health-care increase, we believe that you and your family will benefit significantly from increased control over your own health and well-being. All Canadians can and should have better access to better services in a more timely fashion at a lower overall cost.

2 IMPROVING THE ECONOMIC WELL-BEING OF CANADIANS

Individuals, families, businesses, and non-profit organizations—the four major components of civil society—are free to own, manage, consume, and invest 60% of the nation's Gross Domestic Product (GDP) after governments at all levels have collected tax revenues that enable them to command about 40% of Canada's GDP. It is our contention that quality of life, economic performance, democratic governance, and Canada's international clout would all be strengthened and advanced if the resources available to a free and responsibility-accepting civil society sector were increased to at least two-thirds or 67% of the annual GDP and the governmental share were correspondingly reduced to one-third or 33%.

The principal means for accomplishing this rebalancing of GDP between the governmental and the non-governmental sectors—to dramatically increase the amount of income in the hands of individuals, families, businesses, and NGOs to spend and invest—would be through a long-term overall reduction of the total government burden carried by Canadians of about seven percentage points from present levels, made possible by a combination of spending constraints, reductions, and reallocations at all levels of government.

Figure 4 shows that if the Canadian economy were to grow by just under 5% per year (as predicted by Department of Finance), while the overall annual growth in total government spending were kept to less than 3.1% (which is above the combined rate of predicted inflation and

FIGURE 4: IMPROVING THE ECONOMIC WELL-BEING OF CANADIANS

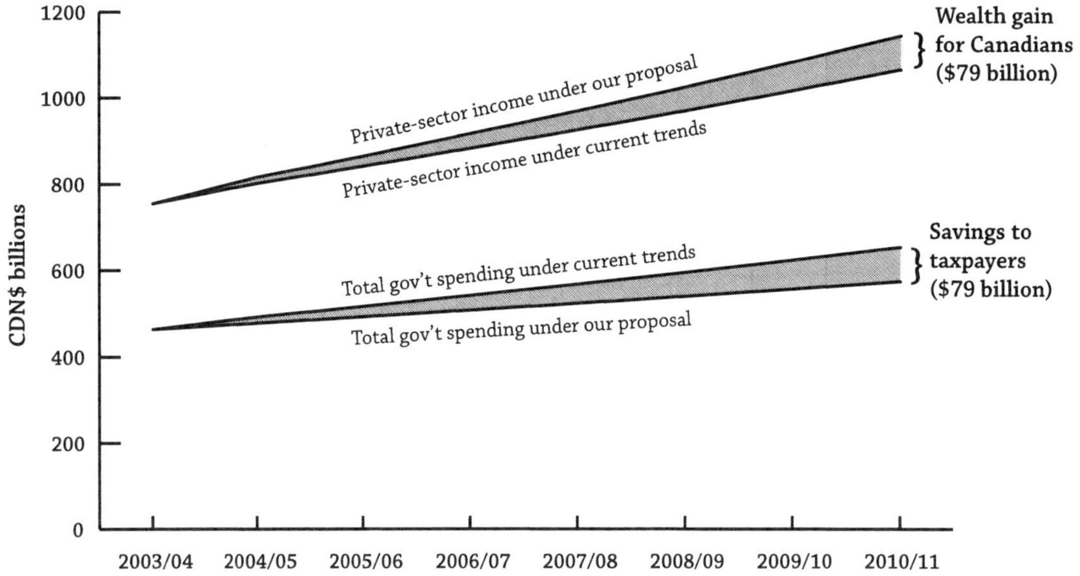

Source: Canada, Dep't of Finance, 2005.

population growth of 2.6% per year), this dramatic increase in the proportion of GDP held by individuals, families, businesses, and NGOs—equal to $79.45 billion—could be accomplished within six years.

In other words, just holding government spending constant in real terms—that is with *no* decrease in government spending—could bring government's share of the economy down to the more desirable level of 33% of GDP in six years, as long as the economy grows at a faster rate than government expenditures. Gains to the private sector could well exceed the $79.45 billion noted above, as tax reductions have a global record of increasing prosperity and employment, as discussed later.

Of course, in practice spending constraints would have to be accompanied by spending re-allocations, with some government programs receiving less money but some receiving more in order to achieve optimal results. Provinces and municipalities, as well as the federal government, would also have to do their part to optimize overall government spending and taxation, particularly since we propose handing back to the provinces their legitimate responsibilities for social services like health care and increased tax room to finance such services

In our future policy paper on Economic Freedom and Responsibility, we will identify and detail specific fiscal and economic policies required to accomplish this rebalancing. We believe that more and more Canadians will be prepared to support such policies if they are genuinely convinced that the current levels of government spending and taxation in Canada are excessive and counterproductive—that such levels of spending and taxation actually do more harm than good to individuals, families, businesses, and the volunteer sector and therefore should be constrained. The following four sections summarize some of the main arguments and facts supporting this proposition.

THE OPTIMAL SIZE OF GOVERNMENT

Economists have long known that government spending follows an upside down "U" curve, like "∩". Initial government spending tends to focus on important government services with high benefits. And as government spending increases, it moves up the left-hand side of the inverted U, with the increasing height representing improvements in well-being. Towards the top, however, benefits decrease with further spending and then begin to decline. Any further increases in well-being produced by further increases in government spending are now more than offset by the income lost by individuals and families, which they could spend more wisely than government to improve their own well-being. In every governmental jurisdiction, there is some point where a dollar *left* in the hands of an individual or business to spend or invest as they see fit—rather than being taxed away—is significantly *more* productive than that dollar in the hands of a politician or government bureaucrat.

In addition, overly high levels of government spending can often be damaging in themselves. For example, O'Farrell (1990) showed that high levels of government spending and subsidies in Nova Scotia had significantly damaged the competitiveness of provincial firms, which had become excessively dependent on government contracts and grants. They could remain highly profitable producing over-priced, low-quality goods for government but were increasingly unable to sell their products in a competitive marketplace. Had they been less dependent upon government and more competitive, they would have created more prosperity and growth for Nova Scotians.

Not surprisingly, economists have spent a great deal of time studying the level of government spending needed to provide citizens with optimal government services. Vito Tanzi and Ludger Schuknecht, for example, in a 1998 paper studied government spending and its effects in 17 industrialized nations. They found that average government spending in these countries rose from 28% of GDP in 1960 to 46% in 1995. They then divided the nations into a "small government" group, with spending under 40% of the economy, and a "big government" group, with spending over 50% of the economy. Significantly, it was the "small" government nations that achieved social and economic performance results (as measured by standard indicators) equal or superior to those of the "big" government nations.

Canada needs an open, honest, and vigorous debate on what is the optimal size of government for this country. Various studies, for example Grubel (1998), suggest that the optimal size of government for mature industrialized countries is around 33% of GDP as compared to roughly 40% for Canada in recent years, as it has come down from higher levels. In other words, government in Canada is too large by a significant margin.

THE HEAVY BURDEN OF EXCESSIVE AND UNFAIR TAXATION

An oversized governmental sector is sustained by levels of taxation that are both excessive and unfair. Currently, the average Canadian household pays more in taxes than for food, shelter, and clothing combined. The average household spends just over $11,715 a year on shelter, $7,045 a year on food, and about $2,245 on clothing, a total of $21,005 a year. Yet, the same average household faces a total tax bill of $27,640 (Veldheis, Emes & Walker, 2003). Put another way, the average household pays a third more in taxes than the total spent on food, clothing, and shelter (see Table 2). In fact, a typical family with two children faces an even greater tax bill, about $35,000 a year.

TABLE 2: INCOME, TAXES, AND SELECTED EXPENDITURES OF THE AVERAGE CANADIAN FAMILY (DOLLARS)

	Average cash income	Total income before tax	Average tax bill	Average expenditures*			Total expenditures
				Shelter**	Food	Clothing	
1961	5,000	7,582	1,675	1,130	1,259	435	2,824
1969	8,000	11,323	3,117	1,497	1,634	654	3,785
1974	12,500	17,976	5,429	2,294	2,320	886	5,500
1976	16,500	21,872	5,979	3,134	2,838	1,119	7,091
1981	27,980	38,758	11,429	5,381	4,440	1,499	11,320
1985	32,309	46,451	14,834	6,984	4,899	2,141	14,024
1990	43,170	60,195	18,693	8,776	5,745	2,234	16,755
1992	44,246	62,791	18,602	9,607	6,024	2,215	17,846
1994	44,720	65,993	19,647	9,592	6,066	2,116	17,774
1996	45,932	68,604	21,148	9,577	6,108	2,017	17,702
1998	48,908	72,193	22,713	10,253	6,048	2,142	18,443
2000	54,283	82,027	26,068	10,630	6,318	2,152	19,100
2002	57,492	86,288	26,696	11,392	6,911	2,294	20,597
2003	58,782	90,458	27,640	11,715	7,045	2,245	21,005

Sources: Statistics Canada, Urban Family Expenditure, catalogue 62-549, 62-547, 62-544, 62-537, 62-535, 62-541, 62-525, 62-555; 1990, 1992, and 1996 Family Expenditure Surveys, catalogue 62-555; 1998 and 2001 Survey of Household Spending; The Consumer Price Index, 62-001-XPB; The Fraser Institute's Canadian Tax Simulator 2003. Adapted from Table 4.4 (page 45) in Veldhuis, Emes, and Walker, 2003.

* All expenditure items include indirect taxes. ** Average Shelter Expenditures for years prior to 1998 are estimates. The estimate is to take account of a change in the definition of shelter between the Family Expenditure Survey and the Survey of Household Expenditures.

These numbers may seem quite large in relation to your actual personal income-tax bill but it is important to remember that we all pay an immense variety of taxes on top of income tax. Every time we buy something, there's the GST and, except in Alberta, a provincial sales tax. Despite falling tariffs, many of the international goods you buy are still taxed by the government at the border and then again with sales taxes. Every time you or your pension account receives a dividend cheque, government has already taken its share through a complicated menu of business taxes. And the list goes on.

Canadians did not always suffer under a tax burden this great. In 1961, the average Canadian household spent less than half as much on taxes as they did on food, clothing, and shelter combined. The tax bill caught up to what we spend on food, clothing, and shelter only in the mid-1970s, but did not consistently exceed these costs until the late 1980s.

Nor is our tax system fair, well-structured, or—as it could and should be—simple to understand. For Canadians, spring should be a season of new beginnings and relief from the tough Canadian winter. Instead, for many Canadian taxpayers, spring is a season clouded with foreboding as the deadline approaches for filing income tax. The most recent study of tax collection and compliance was undertaken for the year 1986 (Vaillancourt, 1989). In that year, governments in Canada spent $771 million to collect taxes and enforce the tax codes' complicated regulations and the private sector spent $4.3 billion in complying with the tax codes, for a total cost of about $5.1 billion. Tax lawyers and accountants are the butt of many jokes and a source of resentment that should be directed at governments in Canada, which promulgate a complicated tax system that keeps tax lawyers and accountants excessively busy.

The complexity of the income tax code and the high cost it imposes on individuals and families in filling out forms or hiring experts to do so—let alone the taxes themselves—should be no surprise. Canada's last major tax reform occurred in the early 1970s. Those reforms still left a complicated system and in the 30 years since then government officials have been busy adding directives, new regulations, loopholes to favour special interests, and further amendments to existing regulations. The very complications of the system give rise to further complications as tax officials attempt to redress the unintended consequences of this complexity, all too often, unfortunately, by writing new regulations rather than simplifying existing ones.

Excessive levels of taxation, excessive complexity—both are made even more onerous by the unfairness of the current tax system. An equitable tax system must meet two requirements, horizontal equity and vertical equity. The Canadian tax system badly fails both tests.

Horizontal equity requires that families with similar incomes should face similar tax bills. The same applies to businesses with similar levels of income. Yet, on the individual and family level, Canada taxes different types of income at different rates. For example, fringe benefits—which bypass many self-employed Canadians and those working in small companies—may not be taxed at all. Income from work is taxed once, income from individual and family investments may be taxed several times, even prior to its being claimed on the family income-tax form.

The same lack of fairness is found in the business world. Some resource industries benefit from favourable tax treatment of special allowances and deductions. Business in Atlantic Canada may benefit from the Atlantic Investment Credit. Complications in various deductions and exemptions benefit some businesses more than others (Wilson, 2003). Other businesses may benefit from subsidies, guaranteed loans, and other taxpayer gifts, which effectively reduce their net taxes, that is, the taxes they pay minus special benefits that are unavailable to other firms that lack political clout to get these favours. The film and other cultural industries gain from any number of tax breaks and special privileges. A company in the film business may face much lower rates of net taxation than a company in, say, the textile business that earns exactly the same amount of money (and may provide jobs to many more people).

Canada's tax system also fails the test of vertical equity: that those with higher levels of income should pay more taxes. For example, a retired couple depending on a modest income from investments may effectively pay higher taxes than an employed couple who have a higher income when their employment income and the value of their benefits are considered. A self-employed family doctor may pay about the same taxes on her earned income as a company manager with the same money income but a higher real income once fringe benefits are considered.

Canada's tax system also discriminates against those families that are primarily supported by one income rather than two. For example, a couple with two children where one partner earns $80,000 will pay about $2,700 more in income taxes than the same family with both partners earning $40,000 each. However, this is not the end of the inequitable treatment. The two-income family can claim a deduction for child care. The one-income family cannot do this if one member of the couple provides child care. This raises the total tax penalty for a family with an at-home parent to about $5,000 a year at this income level (Veldhuis and Clemens, 2004).

HEAVY TAXATION: A NECESSARY EVIL?

Very well, you may say, Canada's tax system is unfair and unnecessarily complex but surely we need to maintain the heavy tax burden—in particular, a heavier burden than our neighbours to the south—in order to fund our menu of government services, particularly health care. The latter part of this claim evaporates immediately on examination. In both Canada and the United States, governments spend just over 6.5% of GDP on health services. Universal health care is not the reason we have high taxes in Canada.

The American health-care system is not a model for reforming Canadian health care. Not only does it fail to provide universal coverage to all citizens but its welter of rules, regulations, and programs makes government's contribution to health-care services in the United States one of the least efficient in the world. Unfortunately, as previously noted, while the Canadian system does provide universal coverage, it too is plagued with gross inefficiencies arising from government monopoly and misallocation of responsibilities among jurisdictions, features that render it less effective and patient friendly than the health-care systems of those nations offering universal coverage through two-track systems. In health care, in both Canada and the United States, we pay too much for what we get.

WHAT WOULD THIS FISCAL REBALANCING MEAN FOR YOU AND YOUR FAMILY?

What would an optimally sized government and reduced tax burden mean for the average Canadian? For illustrative purposes, if in 2003/2004 government spending was equal to 33% of Canada's GDP instead of 40%, the burden of government would have fallen by about $80 billion, for a savings of about $2,500 per Canadian or about $10,000 for a family of four. As previously discussed, this could be achieved in just six years through economic growth, while actually allowing modest increases in real government spending.

But this greatly understates the benefits that Canadians and their families would receive from tax levels commensurate with a size of government that empirical and theoretical research suggests would be optimal. Excessively high tax levels kill jobs and reduce prosperity. Canadians need to understand clearly why Canada's unemployment rate is so consistently high even in good times and why our standard of living is falling relative to that of many of our competitors. A key reason is that we are just not leaving enough dollars in the pockets of consumers to spend, and of businesses to invest in new jobs and wealth-producing activities.

The economic drag caused by high taxes has been known for some time to both economists and well-informed political leaders. For example, in his 1963 State of the Union address, in language that would later be echoed and quoted by Ronald Reagan, President John F. Kennedy said:

> *Our obsolete tax system exerts too heavy a drag on private purchasing power, profits, and employment ... It distorts the use of resources ... This [cutting taxes] is the most urgent task confronting the Congress ...*
>
> President John F. Kennedy, State of the Union Address, 1963

When President Kennedy addressed those remarks to Congress, the total government burden in both the United States and Canada was under 30% of the economy. Since then Canada and the United States have diverged dramatically, with the United State maintaining a government burden of roughly 30% compared to over 40% in Canada. The Kennedy round of tax cuts was passed, though after his death. Remarkably, the growth inducing power of tax cuts was such that within a year total federal tax revenue exceeded what it had been prior to the tax cuts. The same phenomenon would be repeated in the case of President Reagan's tax cuts of the 1980s. Similarly, our tax proposals would enable Canadians to benefit from higher economic growth and lower taxes—and both would dramatically increase the disposable income of Canadians.

For further inspiration, let's quickly take a look at the nation with the most radical experience of tax reform in the western world—that's not Thatcher's Britain or Reagan's United States. In fact, those reforms pale beside the radical changes wrought in Ireland, beginning in the late 1980s. Less than 20 years ago, Ireland was a high-tax nation, with a tax burden even heavier than Canada's. Ireland's unemployment rate was at Newfoundland levels, reaching close to 20% of the workforce. The best and the brightest in Ireland were fleeing to other shores.

Ireland was a desperately poor nation. On a per-person basis, Canada was two and one half times richer than Ireland. Now here's a shocker. Today the average Irish person produces about 20% more wealth than the average Canadian.

Manus O'Riordan, head of research for Ireland's largest union association, the Services Industrial Professional Union once said: "There are whole areas of this city [Dublin] where there is no culture of employment. Taxes are a disincentive to work. We need incentives to work" (McMahon, 2000: 82). Tax reductions in Ireland provided those incentives and today the country is more troubled by labour shortages than job shortages (Chambers of Commerce of Ireland, 2003). Just as Canadians might have been saddened by Ireland's huge numbers of unemployed 20 years ago, the Irish would be appalled by the unnecessarily high unemployment rates Canadians tolerate today. (See Figures 5 and 6 for comparative national data on per-capita GDP and unemployment.)

This dramatic increase in economic well-being—a key objective of our Vision for Canada—was the result of the most radical shift of economic policy that any advanced economy has made in peacetime. Government spending and taxes were reduced, as noted, by far more than they were by Margaret Thatcher or Ronald Reagan. And what was the net result? Astonishing economic growth and a dramatic increase in the Irish standard of living.

Measures to establish government spending and taxation levels, and thus the size of government, at levels that "optimize" quality of

FIGURE 5: GDP PER CAPITA IN CANADA AND IRELAND, CONSTANT LOCAL CURRENCY UNITS

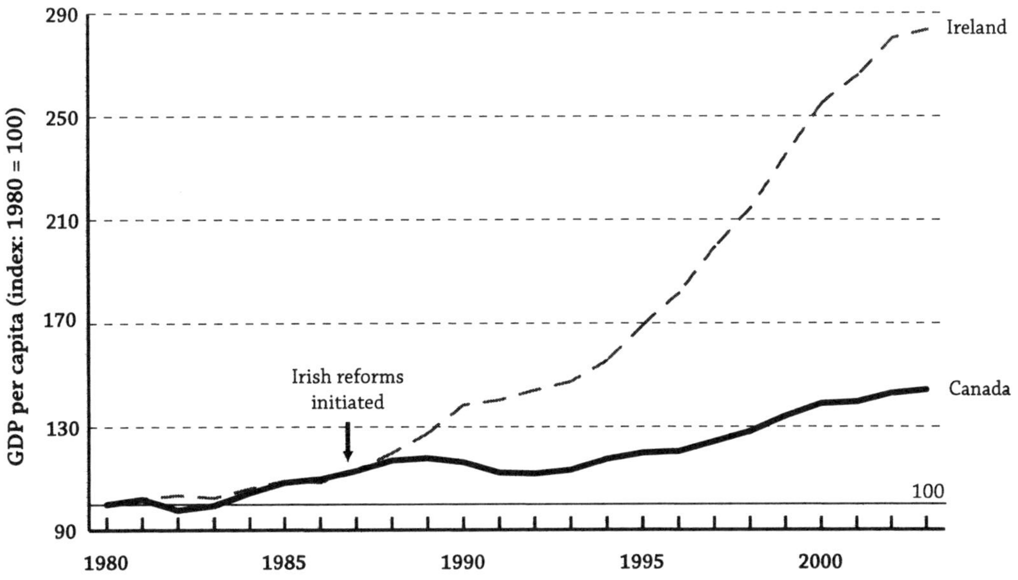

Source: World Bank, 2004.

FIGURE 6: UNEMPLOYMENT IN SELECTED NATIONS, 1980–2002

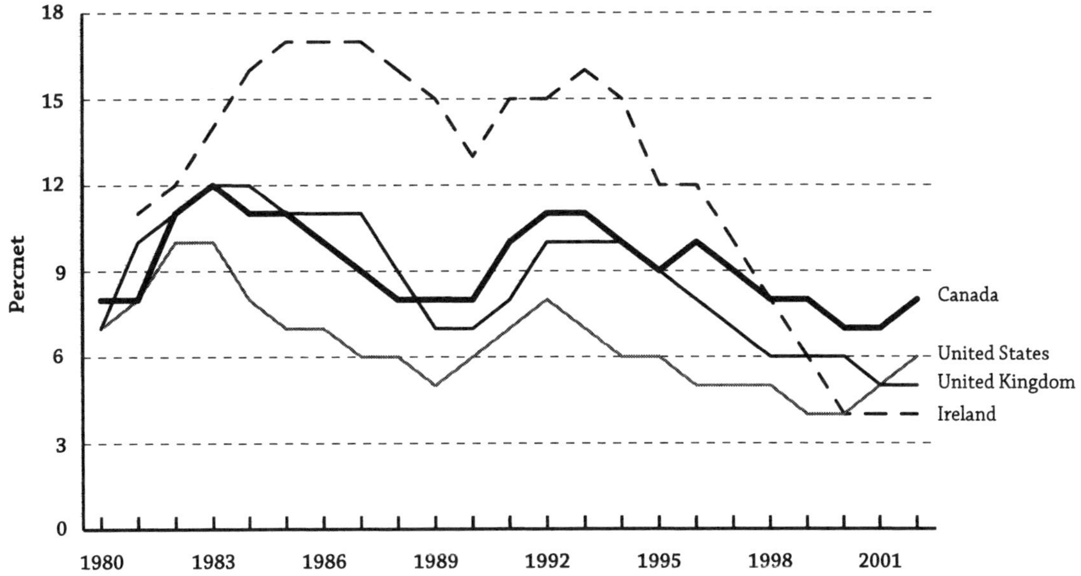

Source: World Bank, 2004.

service and economic growth are not "left wing" or "right wing." They are simply good economic policy. Canadians should ignore ideological labels and resolve to adopt and support sensible economic policies—ones that create jobs and wealth for average Canadians. Quite literally, there is an abundance of evidence throughout the industrialized world that the path to growth, employment, and poverty reduction is found by expanding economic freedom and reducing the weight of government where it has become excessive and counterproductive.

3 OVERCOMING CANADA'S DEMOCRATIC DEFICIT

True freedom of choice and acceptance of responsibility are only possible in a democracy where citizens have the freedom and the responsibility to choose their governments and where they can take action against laws and governments that limit their freedoms. In Chapter 2, we detailed the conditions—all of which exist in Canada—under which citizens become apathetic, indifferent, and even hostile to democratic processes and institutions, and increasingly unwilling to accept responsibility for democratic governance. In a future publication to be entitled "Democratic Freedoms and Responsibilities," we will propose specific policies for alleviating these conditions, including proposals for the reform of democratic processes and institutions, in particular the Parliament of Canada.

In this section, however, we simply want to relate two major points already made to the problem of Canada's democratic deficit. In our judgment, all the procedural and institutional reforms to be proposed to improve Canada's democratic governance will work better and achieve the desired results only if:

- the size of government itself is constrained and reduced as proposed in the sub section above; and

- the responsibilities and resources for public-policy making and service delivery are delegated, wherever and whenever possible, to those levels of governmental organization closest to the people affected by such policies and receiving such services.

In other words, limited and decentralized (localized) government are essential prerequisites to effective democratic governance.

Big, bureaucratic government is by its very nature less amenable to democratic control than limited government. It commands too large a proportion of the nation's resources, it makes too many decisions, it assumes too many responsibilities—thereby restricting the resources, decisions, and responsibilities left in the hand of free and responsible citizens, regardless of the ideology of the party in power or the state of the country's electoral processes and democratic institutions.

Similarly, in a country like Canada characterized by enormous size and diversity, a central government that constantly intrudes on the legitimate responsibilities of the lower levels of government (often in the name of partnerships or decentralization through revenue sharing, but with strings attached) is a threat not an aid to effective democratic governance. It is intrinsically harder (and thus less likely) for citizens to relate to a government that is large and distant—to contact and get to know their representatives, to judge the effects of policies and the quality of services provided, and to hold it accountable—than it is to relate to a government that is smaller and closer at hand.

Virtually all the studies that address the problem of the Democracy Deficit in Canada or abroad focus on reforms to democratic processes and institutions. Our subsequent publication on this subject will have much to say on these subjects also. But we cannot emphasize strongly enough our conviction that the revitalization of democracy in Canada is inseparable from broader economic, political, and constitutional considerations and that no quantum improvement in Canadian democracy can be expected until the size of government in this country is reduced and the responsibilities of government are more decentralized and localized.

4 ADVANCING CANADA'S NATIONAL INTERESTS ON THE INTERNATIONAL STAGE

It may seem odd to propose, as a big, bold idea in foreign affairs, that Canada should vigorously pursue policies that advance the interests of the nation and its citizens internationally. Surely that's what we are doing already. Actually, no. In recent years, the Canadian government has confused preaching shallow sermons about Canada's "values" on the international stage with taking concrete actions to advance Canada's interests internationally. It has been particularly negligent in safeguarding and advancing our most vital international interests—namely our trade and security relationships with the United States, the country that buys more than 80% of our exports, sells us more than 70% of our imports, and provides the continental security blanket under which we reside in peace.

The distinction between promoting values and promoting interests internationally has been well made by the historian J.L. Granatstein. He observes that "Canada is a nation that rarely discusses its national interests" and that "many earnest Canadians might think it abhorrent even to suggest that a country as idealistic and moral as ours has national interests" (Granatstein, 2003). He argues that this failure to distinguish between values and interests is particularly dangerous to Canada when it leads to the mismanagement of our trade and security relationships with the United States.

Two other respected experts on Canada's trade and foreign affairs, Bill Dymond and Michael Hart, make exactly the same points when they describe Canada's foreign policy as "defined by posture, accompanied by a remorseless decline in the respect accorded Canadian interests by US decision-makers and the capacity of Canada to influence US foreign policy" (Dymond and Hart, 2004). While Dymond and Hart were specifically addressing Canada's relationship with the United States, their words apply to the broader canvas of Canada's place in the world.

In a future publication, we will propose specific international trade, defence, and foreign policy initiatives for advancing Canada's national interests in:

- economic prosperity through increased trade;
- security—including preservation of Canada's unity and independence, as well as protection from international threats;
- the protection and advancement of democracy, freedom, economic prosperity, and peace abroad.

In the following paragraphs, we wish to present several important questions and facts that must be addressed in formulating "interest advancing" policy in these areas, and to indicate the direction in which we feel the answers to those questions lie.

CANADA'S TRADE AND SECURITY INTERESTS

Why is it that so many Canadians, including many politicians at the national level, are indifferent or even hostile to our trade relationship with the United States when that relationship is so vital to Canada's economic prosperity?

Not only do we sell about a third of everything we produce to US customers, we also benefit from our immense trade surplus with the United States, more than $100 billion annually or about 10% of our GDP (see Figure 7). At the same time, Canada runs a huge trade deficit with most of the rest of world, including a $19.4 billion with the European Union, a $15.3 billion with Latin America, and $34.4 billion with Asia (see Figure 8). Without US trade, Canadians would scarcely have the means to buy South Korean electronics, Pakistani textiles, French wine, and New Zealand lamb.

It is true of course that Canada has several serious trade disputes with the United States at the present time—for example, with respect to beef and softwood lumber. These have been aggravated and prolonged by protectionist elements in the US and the reluctance of the American administration to confront such interests, especially in election years. Canada must work vigorously to ensure that these disputes are resolved

FIGURE 7: EVOLUTION OF TRADE BETWEEN CANADA AND THE UNITED STATES, 1981–2004

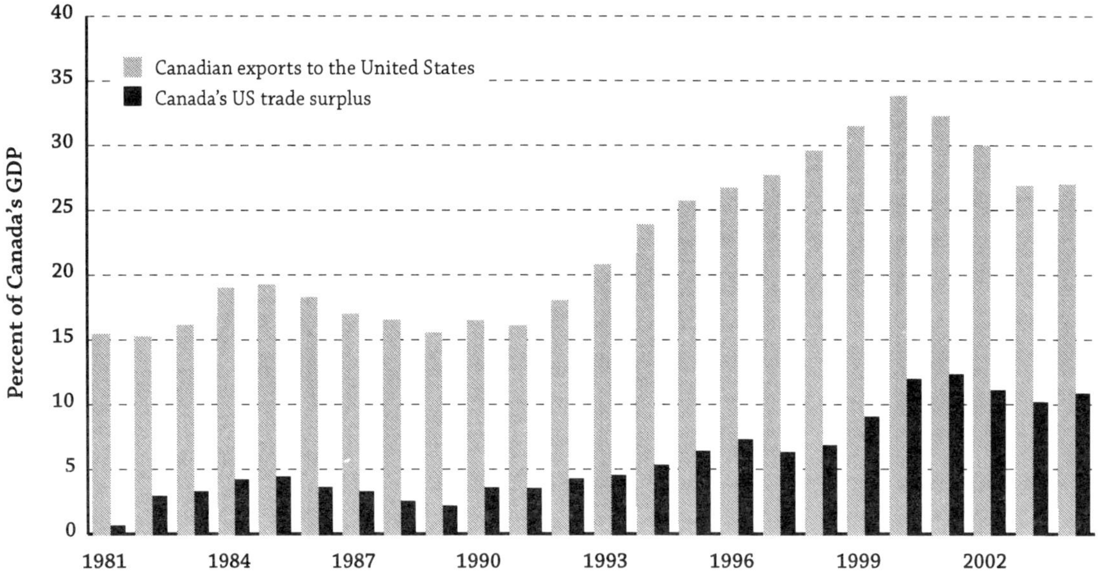

Source: Industry Canada, 2005.

FIGURE 8: CANADA'S TRADE BALANCE, 2004

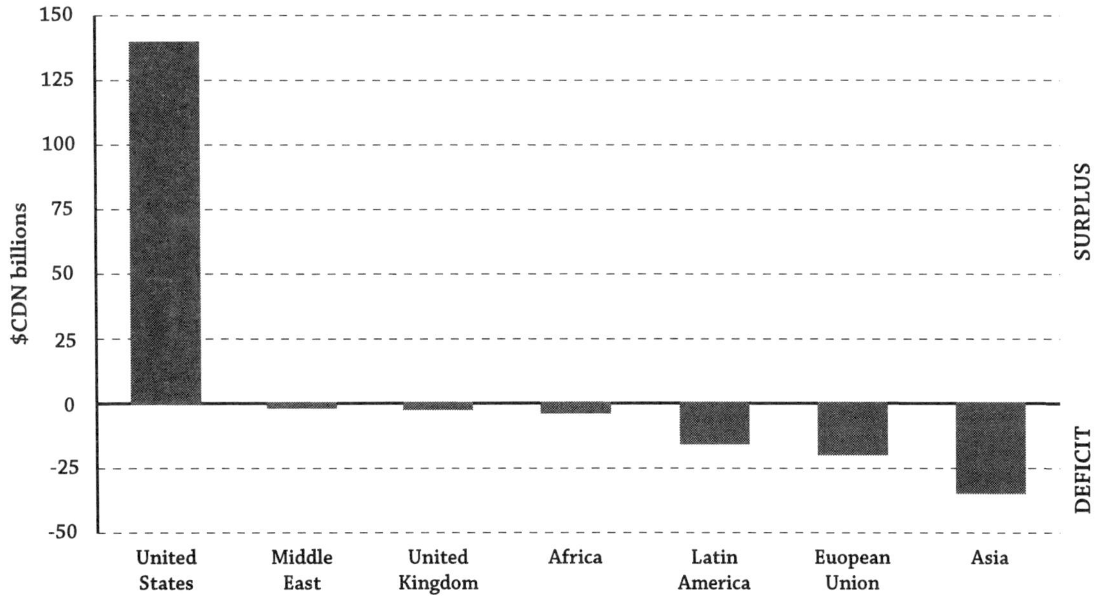

Source: Industry Canada, 2005.

in Canada's favour. But while doing so we should not lose sight of the big picture—that for the most part trade relations between Canada and the United States since 1994 (when NAFTA came into effect) have been surprisingly harmonious, have increasingly contributed to economic prosperity in both countries, and ought to be strengthened and expanded in the future, not weakened or constrained.

Since 1994, when the NAFTA trade dispute settlement mechanism was set up, Canada has faced relatively few US-initiated investigations of our trade practices and has won the majority of our appeals against unfair US trade practices. Over the same period, the European Union has been confronted with five times as many investigations and seven times as many anti-dumping and countervailing "orders" as Canada. Japan's exports to the United States are much smaller than Canada's, but the United States has launched twice as many investigations and six times as many orders against Japan (see Macroy, 2002; Rugman et al., 1999).

Some Canadians discount the contribution of Canada-US trade to Canadian economic prosperity because of the mistaken belief that Canada mainly sends raw materials like oil and gas or semi-processed materials like lumber into the US industrial maw and then buys back manufactured goods, allegedly keeping our manufacturing industry in a weakened state. In reality, American demand drives much of Canada's manufacturing industry—various types of manufactured products being the largest category of our exports to the United States (see Figure 9).

The future expansion of Canada-US trade depends on political leadership and good will, aggressive private-sector marketing, and clear recognition of the mutual advantages of such expansion to both countries. But this expansion, and its protection from crippling disruptions, currently depends very much on something else—the security of the Canada-US border, a security that since 9/11 has been seriously threatened. Canada needs expanded free trade with the United States but it also needs secure trade.

A serious security incident linked to illegal movements of dangerous persons or materials across the Canada-US border would have immediate and damaging effects on trade, and consequently on Canadian jobs

FIGURE 9: CANADA'S EXPORTS TO THE UNITED STATES, 2004

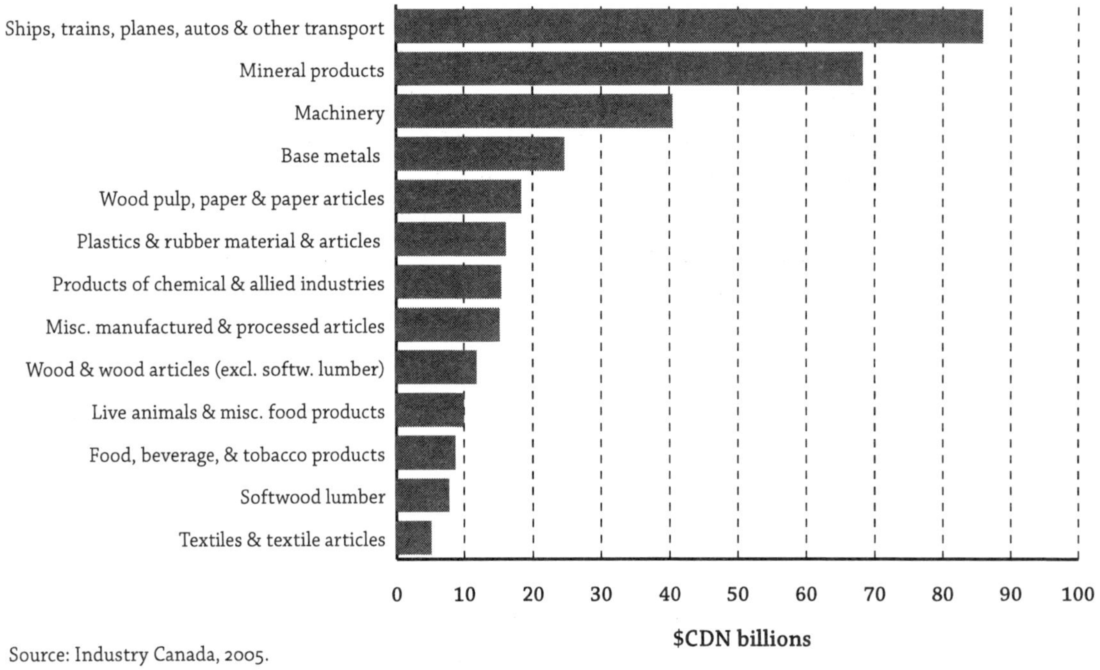

Source: Industry Canada, 2005.

and our standard of living. For example, Goldfarb and Robson (2003) estimate that $141 billion in Canadian exports and 390,000 jobs are presently vulnerable to border disruptions, and $70 billion in exports and 200,000 jobs are indirectly vulnerable.

Much of Canada's high-technology, high value-added industry is focused on the US market and is part of an integrated North American supply and production system with key components on both sides of the border. These industries are particularly vital to the Canadian economy due to the externalities they generate in research, knowledge base, technology transfer, and human capital; and any break-up of the integrated flow of goods and services between them and their American customers would be particularly injurious to them and the jobs, investment, and wealth creation they represent. Trade disruptions due to border-security incidents would be particularly injurious to Canadian firms and workers since Canadian exports to the United States represent about a third of the output of our economy but only a little more than 2% of the output of the US economy. Unlike Canada, the United States would not face as great a disruption to the functioning of its integrated manufacturing system due to a border-security disruption. It is Canada, not the United States, that has the most to lose over such disruptions.

Canada's national interests clearly include expanded free and secure trade with the United States. We consequently believe that to protect and advance these interests for the future, Canada should seek a new Customs Agreement with the United States that would involve the creation of common tariff and quota system and the elimination of rules of origin.

In a future publication, we will deal much more extensively with policies to strengthen Canadian security in other ways—through reform of immigration and refugee policies, expansion of Canada's military resources and capability, and increased cooperation with the US and Mexico on continental defence. But here we are concentrating primarily on the security of the flow of goods and services across the Canada-US border—a security that would be enhanced by a Canada-US Customs Agreement in which Canadian and American officials would mutually administer common tariffs and trade regulations and accept mutual responsibility for any border-security incidents.

The literature on Canada-US relations is sceptical that negotiations to establish a Customs Agreement would be successful in the short run, but does not present any reason to believe that pursuing such an agreement would damage existing trade relations. In fact, if presented as a security measure as well as a trade measure, a Customs Agreement with Canada might get surprisingly good traction in the United States at this time. Certainly, if the negotiation of such an agreement was pursued vigorously and competently by Canada, the contacts, information, and understandings developed through negotiations in good faith might well produce favourable intangibles and, at a minimum, useful side agreements. Such negotiations would also reveal whether it is possible, as we believe it is and as is being demonstrated by the European experience, to maintain national sovereignty while deepening and strengthening trade and economic relations with one's largest and closest trading partner.

CANADA'S INTEREST IN FREEDOM, DEMOCRACY, PEACE, AND PROSPERITY ABROAD

Exactly what is Canada's national interest in promoting human rights and freedoms, democracy, peace, and prosperity abroad, and how serious are we today in advancing that interest in practical ways? On one hand, Canadians, particularly through the work of Canadian-based NGOs and by generous personal giving to international causes, have demonstrated an intense humanitarian interest in the well-being of people in other countries less fortunate than our own. At the same time, this interest is not, nor should it be, entirely altruistic. The spread of freedom, democracy, and peace around the world increases Canada's security. As well, in a global market economy, the prosperity of one nation increases the prosperity of other nations. Increasing prosperity allows individuals and companies in foreign nations to buy more products and services produced here in Canada. Canadian consumers benefit from increased international competition and the improvements that brings in quality and price. Canadians therefore have an undeniable national interest—both humanitarian and self serving—in advancing freedom, democracy, peace, and prosperity abroad.

Canada's interest in protecting and advancing freedom, democracy, and peace abroad is not new—it is a distinguishing characteristic of our national heritage. In the first half of the twentieth century, Canadians felt so strongly about protecting freedom and democracy in Europe and beyond that we were willing to go to war in its defence and more than 100,000 Canadians sacrificed their lives in the First and Second World Wars fighting against tyranny and oppression. In the second half of the twentieth century, it was a Canadian, Lester Pearson, who originated the idea of international peacekeeping through the United Nations. Canada once contributed effectively and substantially—money, personnel, equipment, and leadership—to UN peacekeeping endeavours. We also participated fully in the formation and operations of NATO as a bulwark against the expansion of the tyranny of the old Soviet Union and, with the United States, in protecting North American airspace through NORAD.

But how serious are we today—really—about protecting and advancing freedom, democracy, and peace abroad? The rhetoric is still there, but as the speeches and declarations of our national government leaders on this subject increase in volume and number, and as our lecturing of the United States on the alleged inadequacy and misdirection of its initiatives increases in intensity and moral fervour, the Canadian government's actual willingness and capability to make a substantial and tangible contribution to the international spread of freedom, democracy, and peace abroad has steadily declined.

As previously noted, the strength of our armed forces in terms of military personnel per capita, our percentage of GDP spent on defence, our contributions to NATO and continental defence, and our contributions of money and personnel to international peacekeeping are all at record low levels. We continue to send small contingents of brave and committed Canadian Forces personnel into some of the most dangerous places in the world (although we had to ask the US for help to get Canadian troops and equipment to Afghanistan). But they are inadequately equipped and supported, and their bravery and willingness to serve and act is compromised at the political level at home by ambivalence and cowardice posturing as conviction and prudence.

And how serious are we—really—about tackling poverty and chronic underdevelopment abroad? Traditionally, post-war politicians have pointed to the foreign-aid and related contributions of their governments as a measure of their commitment to this humanitarian goal. But as Granatstein observes,

> *If Canada actually put up sufficient funds to live up to its self-professed image as a caring, sharing nation, we might legitimately be able to press our values on the world. Perhaps. But... we don't provide such support... In 2003 the Centre for Global Development in Washington and the journal* **Foreign Policy** *ranked the 21 richest nations on how their trade, migration, investment, peacekeeping, and environmental policies help or hurt poor nations. Canada ranked 18th.*
> (Granatstein, 2003: 2)

Of course, recent research indicates that foreign aid often does more harm than good and that a more effective strategy for assisting poor countries is through freer trade—that is, by giving them easier access to our markets (see Gwartney et al., 2001; Devarajan, 2001; Easterly, 2003). But again the Canadian government (compromised by its desire to accommodate anti-American, anti-globalization interest groups in Canada) has not been vigorously active in promoting global free trade as a means of helping poorer nations.

So what are the public policies that will effectively advance the interests of Canadians internationally? These, to be explained in detail in a future publication, will include: an international trade policy giving high priority to the pursuit of a Canada-US Customs Agreement; a defence policy that repairs the damage of years of neglect and restores Canada's capability to make real and substantial contributions to continental defence and international peacekeeping; a foreign policy in which the pro-active promotion of global free trade—including increased access for poor countries to Canada's domestic market—largely replaces traditional government-to-government foreign aid; and, above all, an appeal to Canadians to distinguish clearly between their values and their interests, and to pursue the latter with a new honesty and determination on the international stage.

5 THE CHALLENGING ROAD AHEAD

WHAT ACHIEVING THIS VISION WOULD MEAN IN PRACTICAL BENEFITS FOR CANADIANS

Let us assume for a moment that most of the key policy recommendations in the previous section have been adopted with strong public support and actually put into practice. The anticipated benefits to a typical Canadian family include the following.

IMPROVEMENTS IN QUALITY OF LIFE, FOR INSTANCE, WITH RESPECT TO HEALTH CARE

- You will have more freedom to select your own health-care options.
- You will never be forced to wait in a queue because of a government monopoly on health care.
- Your province will have more freedom and resources to provide more timely and higher quality services to its residents.
- The best solutions will be adopted across Canada, particularly those that effectively reduce waiting times and improve quality of care.

IMPROVEMENTS IN STANDARD OF LIVING

- Your taxes will decrease as governments take less money from you and your family.

- You and your family will experience an increase in disposable income and a corresponding increase in freedom of choice and responsibility.

- You and your family will experience better employment prospects and security as the job market strengthens.

- Your standard of living will substantially improve as has that of the residents of those nations that have successfully adopted better public policies.

IMPROVEMENTS IN YOUR EXPERIENCE OF DEMOCRACY AND GOOD GOVERNMENT

- Your province will have its constitutional authority restored to implement the policies that you and the residents of your province deem most important.

- Your federal government will be more effective as it specializes in the responsibilities of a national government.

- Your governments will be more amenable to democratic control as their size is reduced, and as more services are delivered by the government closest to you.

INCREASED CONFIDENCE AND PRIDE IN CANADA'S INTERNATIONAL ROLE

- Your prosperity will be better secured as Ottawa launches new trade initiatives, particularly with the United States, to deepen and expand our international trade.

- Your sense of security will be increased as Canada restores its national and international defence capabilities.

- You will no longer be embarrassed by the failure of Canada's rhetoric to match its actions on the international stage.

- You will be able to take increasing pride in your nation on the world stage as Canada assumes its international responsibilities in defence of freedom and democracy, peacekeeping, and building prosperity in poor nations.

CANADIAN ATTITUDES TOWARD FREEDOM AND RESPONSIBILITY

6 UNDERSTANDING CANADIAN ATTITUDES

Implementation of our Vision for Canada will ultimately depend on the ability and willingness of Canada's political and opinion leaders to understand, clarify, build upon, and challenge various public attitudes and convictions about the expansion of freedom of choice and the acceptance of personal responsibility. To facilitate this process, The Fraser Institute asked Dr. André Turcotte, Professor of Mass Communication at Carleton University and President of Feedback Research Corporation, to conduct a national public-opinion survey of 1500 Canadians during the period from December 3 to 15, 2004. The margin of error for a sample of this size is plus or minus 2.8% with a confidence interval of 95%. Details of these survey results are available at:

www.fraserinstitute.ca/strongandfree or www.fraserinstitute.ca.

FOUR AREAS OF PUBLIC POLICY WHERE CANADIANS WANT MORE FREEDOM OF CHOICE

- 70% of Canadians say they should be allowed to choose any health-care provider they like.
- 55% support the freedom of parents to direct school taxes to the school of their choice, with an even higher percentage (64%) supporting this option if the cost to government is less than that of public schooling.
- 52% of Canadians think that the Canadian economy would perform better if businesses, investors, workers, and consumers had more freedom to conduct their economic affairs as they see fit (that is, if there were less government regulation).

- 68% of Canadians also believe their standard of living would improve if their taxes were reduced rather than increased. This attitude reflects not only a desire for more personal disposable income but also the fact that 64% of Canadians believe they get "less than their money's worth" from taxes paid to governments.

These findings indicate substantial public receptivity to several key components of our Vision for Canada – namely, public policies aimed at expanding freedom of choice in health, education, and the economy and increasing the proportion of national income held by individual, families, businesses, and civil society. Much work remains to be done however to expand and strengthen this desire for freedom of choice in other areas of Canadian life and to resolve various inconsistencies in our attitudes toward freedom and responsibility.

ATTITUDES TOWARD FREEDOM, DEMOCRACY, AND RESPONSIBILITY THAT NEED TO BE FURTHER EXAMINED OR CHALLENGED

While Canadians indicate a desire for greater freedom of choice when presented with specific situations like health-care, education, and the economy, when asked about freedom in a more general and abstract sense—e.g., "Do you feel you have too much, too little, or just enough freedom of choice and control over your life?"—69% say "just enough." This suggests that the proponents of greater freedom of choice in Canadian society should tie their appeals to specific situations—like freedom of choice in social services, life styles, political options, and economic activity—rather than simply appealing to freedom as a principle or abstract notion.

While 70% of Canadians say they should be allowed to choose any health-care provider they like, at the same time 51% say the government allows them enough choice in health-care providers. While 51% of Canadians say health-care services should be provided primarily by governments, 44% say these services should be provided by a mix of public and private providers.

These findings suggest that many Canadians want expanded freedom of choice in health care but at the same time are content with monopoly provision of the service by government—a position that needs to be further examined and challenged for consistency. The strong percentage of Canadians who want health care provided by a mix of pubic and private providers—which is consistent with the high demand for greater freedom of choice in health care—suggests that in future the health-care debate should be focused, not on public care versus private care, but on what is the most appropriate "mix" of public and private service provision and financing for the Canadian health-care sector.

While Canadians appear to be willing to accept an increased degree of personal responsibility for their own wellbeing in a variety of areas (see below), one exception appears to be in the area of environmental conservation. While 31% of Canadians believe they should assume more personal responsibility for protecting the environment, 55% say that this is the government's job. This may mean that Canadians want governments to regulate consumer and producer behaviors detrimental to environmental conservation more strictly. But it also suggests that more work needs to be done to establish a stronger link in the public mind between personal consumption of goods and services and the pressures this creates on the environment—pressures that we can personally alleviate by altering our consumption habits.

While 58% of Canadians are dissatisfied with their ability to influence what governments do between elections—the strongest level of dissatisfaction registered with respect to various aspects of democratic governance covered in the survey—71% professed to be reasonably satisfied with the electoral system, 63% with the way their provincial interests are represented in Parliament, and 59% with the general quality of their representation. These findings appear to suggest that voters see little or no relationship between their inability to control governments between elections and the manner in which their elected representatives are chosen or perform—a view that also needs to be further examined and challenged.

Seventy percent of Canadians think Canada has an obligation to protect rights and freedoms in other countries, with 53% feeling that this obligation must be pursued even if it means sending troops when violent conflicts occur. This is an encouraging sign that Canadians appear to recognize the indivisibility of freedom in an ever shrinking world—that the maintenance of freedom and democracy at home requires a willingness to defend freedom and democracy abroad. More troubling however is the finding that 65% of Canadians feel that Canada's obligation to protect rights and freedoms abroad should be limited to peacekeeping—presumably after someone else has done the dirtier and tougher job of undertaking war missions to establish that peace (i.e., peacemaking). When asked whether Canada should participate in war missions to establish peace, less than 10% answered in the affirmative, with 23% saying, "It depends." Most surprisingly, the responses to this question were virtually the same whether the war missions posed as examples were present-day participation in Afghanistan and Iraq (where Canadian involvement has been minimal) or past participation in World Wars I and II (where Canadian involvement was total). The task for political leadership that would restore Canada to a position of international leadership will involve challenging contemporary Canadian attitudes to peacemaking and converting general public support for peacekeeping into concrete support for measures to increase Canada's peacemaking and peacekeeping capacity.

FIVE AREAS OF PUBLIC POLICY WHERE CANADIANS ARE PREPARED TO ACCEPT MORE PERSONAL RESPONSIBILITY

- 66% of Canadians believe they should take more personal responsibility for their own health. An even higher percentage, 72%, say it is fair to expect those with unhealthy lifestyles to take personal responsibility for additional health-care costs incurred as a result of their lifestyles.

- 56% of Canadians also believe that they should take more personal responsibility for their own education, although only 33% of those between the ages of 18 and 34 share this view.

- 51% of Canadians are prepared to accept more personal responsibility when it comes to providing for their retirement, while 41% say the responsibility should be the government's.

- 51% of Canadians agree that "in order to avoid government limitations on freedom, individuals should take more responsibility for providing for themselves." Stated another way, 41% of Canadians agree with the statement that "individuals should take more responsibility for their own economic well-being," 34% agree that "the government should take more responsibility for the well-being of citizens," with 21% taking a middle-of-the-road position.

- 64% of Canadians say they feel a sense of personal responsibility to improve how democracy is working in Canada, whereas only 29% say this is an area that government should deal with on their behalf. Among Canadians 18 to 34 years of age, 74% say they feel a sense of personal responsibility to improve how democracy is working in this country.

These findings indicate a healthy degree of willingness on the part of Canadians to accept more personal responsibility for their health, education, retirement, and economic well-being—attitudes essential to the acceptance and implementation of responsibility-based public policies. Most encouraging of all is the finding that 74% of Canadians 18 to 34 years of age—the age bracket most frequently associated with political apathy and the "democracy deficit" in developed countries—say that they feel a sense of personal responsibility to improve our democracy. The challenge for visionary leadership will therefore be to translate this professed sense of responsibility into action and support for reforms that will in fact make Canada the best governed democratic federation in the world.

REFERENCES

Canada, Department of Finance (2005). *The Federal Budget 2005*. Ottawa: Department of Finance.

Chambers of Commerce of Ireland (2003). "Chambers Warn of Strain Labour Shortages Are Placing on Business." Dublin, IE: Chambers of Commerce.

Chao, Johnny C.P., and Herbert G. Grubel (1998). "Optimal Levels of Spending and Taxation in Canada." In Herbert G. Grubel, ed., *How To Use the Fiscal Surplus: What Is the Optimal Size of Government?* (Vancouver, BC: The Fraser Institute): 53–68.

Clarke, Rory, and Eileen Capponi (2004). OECD in *Figures: 2004 Edition*. Paris: OECD.

Devarajan, Shantayanan, David Dollar, and Torgny Holmgren, eds. (2001). *Aid and Reform in Africa: Lessons from Ten Case Studies*. Washington, DC: World Bank.

Dymond, Bill, and Michael Hart (2004). "Canada and the New American Empire: Asking the Right Questions." *Policy Options* (June/July): 65–72.

Easterly, William (2003). "Can Foreign Aid Buy Growth?" *Journal of Economic Perspectives* 17, 3: 23–48.

Elections Canada (2004). *Elections Canada: Past Elections* (September 16). Elections Canada Online, <http://www.elections.ca/>.

Esmail, Nadeem, and Michael Walker (2004). *How Good is Canadian Health Care?* Critical Issues Bulletin. Vancouver, BC: The Fraser Institute.

Goldfarb, Danielle, and William Robson (2003). *Risky Business: US Border Security and the Threat to Canadian Exports.* Toronto, ON: CD Howe Institute.

Granatstein, J.L. (2003). "The Importance of Being Less Earnest." C.D. Howe Institute Benefactors Lecture (October 21, 2003), Toronto.

Grubel, Herbert, ed. (1998). *How to Use the Fiscal Surplus: What Is the Optimal Size of Government?* Vancouver, BC: The Fraser Institute.

Gwartney, James, Chuck Skipton, and Robert Lawson (2001). "Trade Openness, Income Levels, and Economic Growth." In James Gwartney and Robert Lawson, *Economic Freedom of the World: 2001 Annual Report* (Vancouver, BC: The Fraser Institute): 71–87.

Industry Canada (2005). *Trade Data Online.* <http://strategis.ic.gc.ca> (as of March 11, 2005).

International Institute for Strategic Studies (2002). *The Military Balance* 2002–2003. London: Oxford University Press.

McMahon, Fred (2000). *Road to Growth.* Halifax, NS: Atlantic Institute for Market Studies.

O'Farrell, P.N., in association with Gardner Pinfold Consulting Economists Ltd. (1990). *Small Manufacturing Competitiveness and Performance: An Analysis of Matched Pairs in Nova Scotia and New England.* Commissioned by the Nova Scotia Department of Industry, Trade and Technology, and Atlantic Canada Opportunities Agency.

Pammett, Jon H., and Lawrence LeDuc (2003). "Explaining the Turnout Decline in Canadian Federal Elections: A New Survey of Non-voters." Ottawa: Elections Canada.

Statistics Canada (2001). *Population Projections for Canada, Provinces, and Territories 2000–2026*. Ottawa: Statistics Canada.

Tanzi, Vito, and Ludger Schuknecht (1998). "Can Small Governments Secure Economic and Social Well-Being?" In Herbert Grubel, ed., *How to Use the Fiscal Surplus: What Is the Optimal Size of Government?* (Vancouver, BC: The Fraser Institute): 69–92.

United States Bureau of Labour Statistics (2005). *Foreign Labour Statistics*. <http://data.bls.gov/> (as of March 7, 2005).

Vaillancourt, Francois (1989). *The Administrative and Compliance Costs of the Personal Income Tax and Payroll Tax System in Canada, 1986*. Canadian Tax Paper No. 86. Toronto, ON & Montreal, QC: Canadian Tax Foundation.

Veldhuis, Neils, and Jason Clemens (2004). "Does Canada Have a Marriage Tax Penalty?" *Fraser Forum* (March): 9–12.

Veldhuis, Neils, Joel Emes, and Michael Walker (2003). *Tax Facts 13*. Vancouver, BC: The Fraser Institute.

Wilson, Thomas A. (2003). "An Evaluation of Business Taxes in Canada." In Herbert Grubel, ed., *Tax Reform in Canada: Our Path to Greater Prosperity* (Vancouver, BC: The Fraser Institute): 111–38.

World Bank (2004). *World Development Indicators Online*. <http://www.worldbank.org/>.